Bible
Reading
for
Spiritual
Growth

Bible Reading *for* Spiritual Growth

A HARPERCOLLINS RESOURCE
FOR SMALL GROUPS AND INDIVIDUALS

Norvene Vest

■ HarperSanFrancisco
A Division of HarperCollins*Publishers*

BIBLE READING FOR SPIRITUAL GROWTH. Copyright ©
1993 by Norvene Vest. All rights reserved. Printed in the
United States of America. No part of this book may be used
or reproduced in any manner whatsoever without written per-
mission except in the case of brief quotations embodied in
critical articles and reviews. For information address
HarperCollins Publishers, 10 East 53rd Street, New York,
NY 10022.

FIRST EDITION

Library of Congress Cataloging-in-Publication Data
Vest, Norvene.
Bible reading for spiritual growth : a HarperCollins
resource for small groups and individuals / Norvene Vest.
— 1st ed.
p. cm.
Included bibliographical references.
ISBN 0-06-068957-9 (pbk.)
1. Bible—Devotional use. 2. Bible—Reading.
3. Spiritual life—Catholic Church. 4. Church group work.
5. Catholic Church—Membership. I. Title.
BS617.8.V47 1993
220'.07—dc20   92-53913

93 94 95 96 97 98 ❖ CWI 10 9 8 7 6 5 4 3 2 1

Contents

Introduction

Many of us experience a deep thirst for a meaningful spiritual life. We find ourselves touched by the haunting image in Psalm 42:1–2:

> As a deer longs for flowing streams, so longs my soul for you. O God. My soul thirsts for God, for the living God.

We feel the need for genuine spiritual refreshment as we wander through an environment all too often parched and dry. We long for an affirming relationship with God that will make a difference in how we experience daily life. We eagerly set out on the inviting journey of spiritual growth, seeking deeper relationship with God's very self.

We may indeed begin such a journey, doing some reading, joining some worship, trying to live attuned to God's presence. Yet before we are very far along, we discover that we cannot go it alone. We need help, advice, and guidance. We need the plentiful wisdom that comes from others well-advanced in this spiritual journey. Yet there are not many such souls immediately available to most of us, so we may begin to feel discouraged and abandoned. Sometimes it seems that our search for spiritual growth serves more to emphasize our dryness than to lead us to waters of refreshing coolness.

In particular, we may be disappointed by a foundational resource, the Bible, which our spiritual ancestors seem to have found fruitful. Turning to the Holy Scriptures of the Judeo-Christian tradition, we may occasionally find ourselves bewildered, disappointed, or sometimes downright alienated by what appears to be experience so far removed from our own that we cannot find any way to unlock its value. Is the living, compassionate God revealed in Scripture in a way that offers guidance and comfort to us in the issues of daily life? The conviction offered in this book is that Scripture does indeed so reveal God! There is even a time-honored method to reading the Bible that teaches us specifically to encounter God in that way. This book shows how our Scriptures can genuinely and consistently aid our spiritual growth, rather than seeming only to be another dry well.

The simple process of reflection on the Bible that is presented here is intended specifically for spiritual nourishment. We often think of reading the Bible as a process of study. But there is a way of reading the Bible *devotionally*, for spiritual thirst. Christians have long known a means of turning to Scripture that transcends any time- and culture-specific references, reaching into the reader's present experience to facilitate spiritual growth.[1] Yet this older process has been set aside in the "rational" centuries since the Enlightenment—the definitive split that had emerged between sacred and secular in philosophy and the arts, politics and economics, social structure and daily life by the end of the eighteenth century.

In general, our post-Enlightenment twentieth century tends to emphasize an historical and analytical approach toward any text, and many gains have been achieved with this approach. Systematic analysis of the Scripture has yielded valuable insights about events at the time of writing, the relationship between various editors, and the like. But such details have tended to overwhelm a more devotional method of simple waiting in the presence of God in Scripture. The older tradition viewed the Bible as an aid to the spiritual life rather than chiefly as a source of information.

Yet, even though it is difficult for us now to imagine what a devotional approach to the Bible might mean, much less how to go about it, the ancient Christian art of Bible reading for spiritual growth has never been totally lost. Today this approach is gradually reemerging in several radically different Christian settings, from monastic communities in the United States to recently evangelized African Christians. This book offers a means of Bible reading for spiritual growth available to all.

The ancient Christian tongue-twister name for the simple process on which we base our method is *lectio divina* (pronounced lex-ee-oh di-vee-nuh). This Latin phrase translates literally into English as "divine reading," and refers primarily to the reading of sacred Scriptures as practiced by the early Christian fathers and mothers. In Latin as in

English, the adjective "divine" refers both to the material being read (the divine Word) and the method of reading (an inspired approach). The Latin also carries a tradition of meaning that is more vast than can be suggested in the literal English translation. Therefore, we continue to use the Latin phrase, and usually abbreviate it simply as "lectio."

Historically, lectio is used by both individuals and groups, with much variation in actual practice. It is focused on the good word of God as revealed in divine Scriptures, although it can also be practiced on other books of great spiritual depth, and even with content drawn directly from life. Lectio looks to the Bible as the genuine word of God, a privileged text in which Christians are continually nourished in faith. Yet, it is not Bible *study*, for it does not involve analysis of a scriptural passage nor emphasis on information about the text. Scripture study is an essential supplement to ongoing lectio, but is not directly involved in this process. Above all, lectio is undertaken in the conviction that God's word is meant to be a "good" word—that is, something carrying God's own life in a way that is beneficial to one who receives it faithfully. Lectio turns to the Scripture in order that we be nourished, comforted, refreshed by it. Lectio is an encounter with the living God. It is prayer.

Yet it is a different mode of deep prayer than much modern practice. It involves reason and discursive thought, an inner exploration of meaning. It connects daily prayer with both the creedal truths of the Christian tradition and the current issues life presents. In lectio, we are fully engaged, with mind and body as active partners in spiritual nourishment. There is an active mode to lectio, as well as a receptive mode, and both are essential to its practice. For example, the central meditative phrase which comes from the Scripture passage to each of us in Lectio is not the same as a mantra, which is intended to still mental thought in order to deepen spiritual centering. On the contrary, the content of the unique, short lectio phrase is seen as a gift, enabling direct interaction with the actual situations of our lives, evoking new images and possibilities that empower us to live congruent with our faith. The central lectio phrase is the fruitful word of God, in the sense Isaiah intends:

For as the rain and snow come down from heaven, and do not return
there until they have watered the earth, making it bring forth and sprout,
giving seed to the sower and bread to the eater; so shall my word be that
goes out from my mouth; it shall not return to me empty, but it shall accomplish that which I purpose and succeed in the thing for which I sent
it. (Isaiah 55:10–11)

The Group Approach to Lectio Practice

As used here, lectio is a process of group Bible reflection. This book
presents a particular frame for the ancient art of Bible reading for spiritual growth—that of a group setting and a careful sequence of simple steps. The basic process for our group lectio is roughly this: The
leader reads a short passage from Scripture, and in silence the group
members listen attentively for a particular word or phrase that seems
to be given to each. Then, each simply speaks aloud the word received.
Another member reads the same passage a second time, and in silence
the group members ponder how the passage seems to touch their lives.
Then, each person briefly speaks aloud his or her sense of being
touched. The same passage is read a third time, and in silence the
group members reflect on a possible invitation found in the passage
to do or be something in the next few days. Each person speaks of the
invitation he or she has received. Finally, the group members each pray
that the person to the right be empowered to do or be what he or she
feels called to do or be.

Lectio connects prayer with daily life. So it is natural that the lectio process should involve not only a sense of being touched by the
Scripture passage, but also of receiving an invitation that expresses
some integration with daily life. However, lectio's contribution to life
may often be expressed by some form of not-doing, rather than by
doing more. Our lives frequently are overloaded already, and God's invitation may well be to rest, to set aside all our doings for a time, to
be nourished and receive nurture. Thus the form of lectio's invitation
is *to be* as well as to do. For example, today's lectio invitation may be to
be less impatient, or to be attentive to the crisp smell of autumn out-
doors. Often it is a great relief to realize that God is not asking us to

do something (more), but is rather inviting us to *experience* the loving embrace which already surrounds us.

This process of group lectio involves a communal expression of the deep personal intimacy with God that is at the heart of Christian faith. By and large, those of us who experience such intimacy seldom express it, much less in a group setting. We think of intimacy with God as being so personal that it might seem "indecent" to share it. Certainly, some risk is involved in such faith-sharing, so such sharing is never forced. On the contrary, any verbal contribution is regarded as a gift to the group, and is never demanded. And gradually, as the group experiences the beauty of the inner life of Christ appearing so powerfully in the context of each broken and incomplete human life, a natural and deepened mutual reverence grows among the members. Sharing about intimate experience of God—when offered freely and not demanded—enables us all to become more fully who we are. Our reverence for Christ's life experienced in each other is bound to overflow to a new and more accepting perspective about our humanity, even our own.

You might have reservations about undertaking this process without some sort of professional leadership. Perhaps you feel that any meaningful group interaction with Scripture needs to be facilitated by someone "knowledgeable." Or maybe you have attended occasional "self-led" groups that seemed merely to pool the participants' ignorance or offer a forum for a sustained harangue from a single—if well-meaning—point of view. You may think that any reading of the Bible inevitably needs to teach objective and dogmatic truths of the gospel, which requires formal leadership.

Lectio needs to be rooted within a context of access to and study of objective information about Scripture, and of ongoing participation in a Christian community in which principles of faith are emphasized. But lectio itself is not primarily a process of knowledge acquisition, nor about mastery of truth. Instead, lectio is primarily a process of encounter; it is about surrender to Truth. It is a seeking of God and God's own word within the Scripture. In this sense—that of present and living encounter with a transforming God—there are no experts, there is no end to knowledge, as Psalm 139 suggests:

> How weighty to me are your thoughts, O God! How vast is the sum of them! I try to count them—they are more than the sand; I come to the end—I am still with you. (Ps. 139:17–18)

Thus, formal or professional leadership is not necessary for lectio. Effective lectio stems principally from silent attentiveness to the word of Scripture in relation to the specifics of each individual life. Effective lectio emphasizes openness to personal encounter at the unique intersection of life and Scripture. The primary "information" needed for lectio is the actual situation in each person's own life. The primary disposition needed for lectio is willingness to offer this life-information for dynamic interaction with God's word heard by each person within today's Scripture.

Lectio is designed to facilitate an encounter with the living God, in such a way that we are gradually transformed into Christ's own likeness. It is intended to enable us to release the barriers and blind spots that separate us from God and prevent us from becoming the person God continually calls each of us to be. It is intended to empower us to reconcile the world to God in Christ, becoming peacemakers and agents of justice in every arena of our lives.

Many of us have no idea how to grow into the likeness of Christ. We have no conception of any means that might assist us to unfold in the spiritual growth promised to us in baptism. We have not experienced reading the Bible as a powerful means of personal spiritual transformation. *Lectio enables this change.* It is a potent instrument, one that both acknowledges our limitations and enables us to transcend them in Christ. It enables us to become the children of God we long to be. It enables us to slake our thirst for God in the flowing streams of Scripture given to us for that purpose.

The Book's Content

This book is designed as a guide—a practical vehicle showing how small Christian groups can meet with lectio practice at their center. The participants might be members of a parish or a congregation, or they might be oblates in a monastic community, or groups formed ad hoc by Christians sharing work or volunteer committees who desire to meet together with Christ at the center. Group members provide support, strength, and accountability to one another, as guided by the Holy Spirit, for the difficult work of being Christians in the midst of the world.

The chapters are designed to help groups begin and continue successful lectio practice together, anticipating questions that might arise, and offering helpful supplemental information. Chapter 1 sets forth the group lectio process as offered here for group use. First the process is described. Then an example is given of an imaginary group experience, as it might actually happen. (We follow that imaginary group throughout the book.) Finally, a summary chart is presented for quick reference.

Chapters 2, 3, and 4 discuss three different aspects of lectio practice. Chapter 2 covers the heart and rhythm of the practice, particularly in light of its underlying structure, which is sometimes at variance with implicit assumptions of twentieth century western culture. Chapter 3 establishes basic guidelines—the nuts and bolts, as it were—of actually getting a group under way. Chapter 4 offers advice on how to select good texts for group lectio practice, and presents some good, central texts for use in the beginning.

Chapter 5 extends the range of lectio for those who are interested. Since lectio is intended to shape our ways of seeing and responding to the world, it is suggested that the "texts" we use for the lectio method of encounter with God might be expanded to include incidents that occur in daily life. The theory is presented with a sample practice and a summary chart.

Chapter 6 presents background information on the heritage and worldwide scope of Christian lectio practice. The Epilogue offers examples of personal transformation, the expression of spiritual growth, which is the intended outcome of lectio and the goal of our hearts.

CHAPTER 1

The Process of Lectio Divina in Groups

Lectio divina is a powerful means of Bible reading for spiritual growth. This book shows how to practice lectio with a Christian small group— a method that is a synthesis of many sources (these sources are discussed in chapter 6). Some may find they have already been practicing a devotional approach to Scripture very like this, but with a different name. Others may find they already practice lectio, but in a slightly different format than that presented here. The method presented here is both faithful to the tradition and responsive to contemporary needs.

This first chapter presents our specific group lectio method by outlining and discussing the basic procedure. Each step of the process is described, and then a realistic example of a group experience is given. A summary chart is presented at the end of the chapter for reference.

This is the group lectio procedure, stated briefly:

> After a period of preparation, the leader reads a short passage from Scripture. In silence, the group members listen attentively for a particular word or phrase that seems to be given to each. Then each person simply speaks aloud the word he or she has received.

> A member other than the leader reads the same passage a second time, and in silence the group members ponder how the passage seems to touch their lives. Then one by one they briefly speak aloud their sense of being touched.

> The same passage is read a third time, and in silence the group members reflect on what the passage seems to be

inviting them to do or be over the next few days. Then the members each speak of their invitation.

Finally, each member prays that the person to the right will be empowered to do or be what he or she feels called upon to do or be.

Let's look at this process now in more detail, with examples.

Preparation

The group gathers, sitting in a close circle. Only the leader has a Bible, with a passage of no more than ten verses selected. The leader begins by aiding the group members to become quiet and fully present, in expectancy of hearing and receiving God in their midst. It is well to take a few moments to relax, releasing tensions and preoccupations and becoming attentive to what will be heard. It is also helpful to sit upright, comfortable yet alert, to close the eyes and focus on breathing, and to spend a few moments in silence before anything else occurs.

EXAMPLE

Three couples from Immanuel Church have been meeting once a week for dinner. They have been doing this for several months, and recently decided that they want a focus for their faith-sharing, so they have committed to do lectio together before their weekly dinners. Tonight's meeting is at the home of Sharon and Charles. The other two couples, Bill and Mary and Jim and Ann, have arrived and put their potluck dishes in the kitchen. The children are settled in the basement family room, under the supervision of a neighbor's teenage daughter, whom they are paying to babysit while they meet.

Now the group has gathered in a close circle, and Sharon convenes them as leader for the evening. She begins by inviting everyone to "simmer down" and set aside all their distractions, exhaling all physical tensions and having a few moments of quiet, focusing on breathing.

Stage One: Hear the Word

The leader reads the selected passage twice. The first time helps the group members orient themselves to the particular passage; they can listen for overall comprehension. The second reading, immediately following, is a bit slower. This time members are invited to listen attentively for a particular word or phrase that seems especially to attract them at the moment. It must be a word or phrase from the *passage itself*, yet it need not be at all central to the passage. For example, if the passage begins "Jesus went across the lake in the boat with his disciples to pray," it may be that the word that particularly seems to call to you at the moment is *boat*. You do not need to understand why, nor explain or defend the choice of word either to yourself, to the group, or to God. You would simply consent to receive the word *boat*. Then you would repeat it softly over and over to yourself in the minute of silence following the reading.

The group members wait to speak until the leader invites all of them to say the word or phrase they have specially heard. It is important that no one explain or elaborate on what has been heard; each person says only the word or phrase received from the passage, without additional comment. Also, at any stage anyone may choose not to share but to pass, for any reason or no reason. So at this time, each member either speaks his or her word or phrase or indicates a desire to pass.

EXAMPLE

Sharon has chosen a passage from the Gospel of John (1:35–39), which she reads aloud, as follows:

> The next day John again was standing with two of his disciples, and as he watched Jesus walk by, he exclaimed, "Look, here is the Lamb of God!" The two disciples heard him say this, and they followed Jesus. When Jesus turned and saw them following, he said to them, "What are you looking for?" They said to him, "Rabbi" (which translated means Teacher), "where are you staying?" He said to them, "Come and see."

Sharon then reads the passage again, first asking the group members to listen for a word or phrase from the passage that seems to call out to them or have a special attraction. When she is finished reading, she asks them to repeat their word or phrase to themselves softly, over and over, for one minute. At the end of the minute, Sharon invites each of them in turn to speak aloud *only* the word or phrase they heard, or to pass. Charles says, "teacher." Ann says, "followed." Mary says, "come and see." Bill says, "what are you looking for?" Jim passes. Sharon says, "come and see."

Stage Two: How Is My Life Touched?

The leader asks another person in the group to read the passage for the second stage of the process. It is well to choose a variety of voices to read during a lectio session because different voices often lead us to hear different things. This time the passage is read only once, slowly.

Before this reading begins, the leader reminds the group that they are to listen to the passage with the particular question in mind, "How is my life touched by this passage today?" And they should continue this contemplation in the two to three minutes of silence that follow. Normally, this question is pondered specifically in relation to the word or phrase found during the first stage, but this is not rigid. Another word or phrase may substitute itself in this second listening.

The members may consider the question "How is my life touched . . ." in one of two ways. The first way is our normal, abstract way of understanding, for example, "Considering that my life is a constellation of specific matters at the moment, and the Scripture passage is also a constellation of factors, in what ways do the two seem to inform and interact with each other?" The second way is more sensory and less abstract. That is, you can interpret the word *touched* more literally, and allow yourself to be receptive to a special image, sound, taste, touch, or smell that seems to be given in relation to the passage. You may not immediately understand what the connection is between, for instance, the image that emerges and the passage itself, but again, you consent simply to accept what is given and to dwell with it and reflect on it during the silence following the reading.

As before, the leader brings the silence to a close by inviting members to share *briefly* (one or two sentences) how they sense their lives to be touched by the passage. Members might begin with a phrase such as "I hear," "I see," or "I sense," and continue for one or two sentences. It is again quite important that the words shared be succinct, without explanation or justification of what has been sensed. And again, anyone may choose to pass.

EXAMPLE

Sharon asks Bill to read the passage, and he starts immediately. She gently interrupts him, and says she would like to give a word or two of guidance before the group listens to the Scripture again. "This time," she says, "we are listening to the passage with the question in mind, 'How is my life touched by this passage?' We may receive a 'sensory' touch. For example, a sight or sound may come to mind. In contrast, we may have an idea about a connection between the passage and our lives. There will be about two minutes of silence for reflection after the reading." She asks Bill to begin, and he reads the passage.

After two minutes of silence, Sharon invites members to share *briefly* how they have sensed their lives touched, perhaps beginning "I hear . . . " or "I see. . . ."

Ann says, "I see a dusty road, very hot and dry, and in the far distance, a figure dressed in white, whom I am somehow following."

Charles says, "I see Robin Williams in *Dead Poets Society*, leading his class out into the hallway to look at photos of long-dead students and urging them to seize the day." He gives an embarrassed laugh, but does not explain further.

Mary says, "My phrase was 'come and see,' but I didn't see anything, although I seem to hear a fountain gurgling. I guess I'm not doing it right."

Jim breaks in, "Of course you're doing it right. It's just a ridiculously awkward process!" Sharon smiles and signals them both to an uncomfortable silence.

Bill looks up, as if coming back from a long distance, and says, "That phrase just keeps haunting me—what am I seeking, what do I *really* want?

I realize that it has been years since I even thought about such a question. Do I really want to be vice-president of my firm, if it means never seeing my kids go to bed!" He shakes his head and lapses into silence.

After a period of silence, Sharon asks, "Jim, would you like to pass or share?"

Jim says, "It's obvious that all of us have to let Jesus be our leader and give us direction."

After a moment, Sharon says, "My phrase was 'come and see,' and I feel there is a grown-up taking my hand, with me as a child, and walking with me to the side of a great meadow, full of beautiful yellow flowers. It is so lovely!"

Stage Three: Is There an Invitation Here?

The leader asks another person in the group to read the passage for the third stage of the process. Before the reading begins, the leader reminds the group that while they listen to the passage, and during the two to three minutes of silence that follows, they should think about the question "Do I sense that this passage is inviting me to do or be something in the next few days? Is there encouragement or an invitation to me here, not so much for some long-term project, but for something I might do or be in the next day or two? Concretely, what do I sense this passage is calling me to do or be right now?"

The designated person then reads the passage once, slowly, and the members of the group ponder this invitation in two to three minutes of silence. Then once more the leader brings the silence to a close by inviting members to share whatever they sense from the passage. This time the sharing may be at somewhat more length, as each participant desires. During this sharing, members pay particularly close attention to what the person to their right says, since they will each pray for that person when the sharing is complete. Once again, anyone who wishes may pass.

The group's responsibility is to receive whatever is shared respectfully and prayerfully, without comment. Probably there will be a keen sense of God's presence, and by respectful listening, the group indicates its confidence that each speaker is being cherished by God in this very moment, however joyful or painful, sorrowful or confused, loved or lost the speaker feels.

EXAMPLE

Sharon asks Ann to read this time, and before Ann begins, Sharon briefly instructs the group: "This time we are listening to the passage with the question in our minds, 'Do I sense here an invitation to do or be something in the next few days?'—not meaning by the end of your life, but just in the next week or so. 'Is there something I am invited or encouraged to do or be?'" Ann then reads the passage, and there is silence.

Sharon brings the silence to a close by asking the group to share, at more length if they wish, anything each feels invited to do or be by the passage. She also reminds them that they may pass if they prefer.

There is another twenty seconds of silence, then Charles says hesitantly, "I am struck by the fact that Jesus is called 'Teacher' here. This last month I've been really struggling with whether to stay with high school teaching or to try for a job that pays more and has less personal stress. You all know that I feel this school district is a nightmare of political maneuvering and they don't really value their teachers. What might it mean to be a teacher like Jesus was? I don't feel I'm getting any *answers* from the passage, but I *do* want to ponder these questions seriously over the next week: 'What does it mean to be a teacher like Jesus was?' and 'Could I do that?'"

Bill responds, "Boy, does that ever make sense to me! My word was 'what do you want?,' and that really applies in spades to my situation right now. I just don't know what I want . . . or maybe I want it all! I've got a responsibility to bring in enough income to support my family, and I really get a kick out of the challenges in the banking industry, but these long days and frequent trips take all my energy. I feel like a money-making machine; I never get to *enjoy* Mary and the kids! Maybe it is unrealistic to want to do that. All I see to do is keep on doing what I'm doing."

Jim looks like he's about to give Bill some advice, but Sharon motions to him to wait. After a few moments of silence, Mary says, "I'm in such a different place. The fellows seem to be so logical and articulate, but for me it's more personal. I was thinking about John the Baptist sending his disciples away to Jesus, and it made me want to cry. You work so hard to get a little acknowledgment of your own value, and then before you've had a chance to appreciate it, you have to give it away! It's *John* who I want to come and see, to talk about what it's like to have to give up something precious. I choose to do that—to have an imaginative talk with John the Baptist!"

Ann's eyes are filling with tears. She opens her mouth a couple of times before words will come, then mumbles, "Jesus is so far away, and it's such a struggle to follow him." She says no more and her tears are under control now. Mary reaches out and squeezes Ann's hand. Sharon murmurs something about "the gift of tears in God's presence."

Jim is looking uncomfortable. He snorts out, "Pass."

Sharon says, "I often find things too difficult or confusing for me to really know what to do—even leading this lectio, for example. But I guess the invitation I sense for myself is to stay with Jesus, to keep my hand in his, and to walk forward into the difficulty or confusion as best I can, watching to see what he will do."

Stage Four: Prayer

When all have shared or passed, the leader begins the time of prayer. He or she reminds the group that although only one person at a time is formally praying, that person is praying on behalf of the whole group, who jointly hold up the person in prayer before God. It is helpful for each person to say Amen when his or her prayer is finished, and for the group to echo that Amen to reinforce the awareness that it is the whole group's prayer at every moment.

The purpose of the prayer is very simple: that this person may be empowered by God to do or be what was sensed as invitation. The one praying may also include a few words of personal thanksgiving for the brother or sister to the right, but at this time, the prayer's focus is simply on acknowledging that the individual's desire is supported by the prayers of all the others present and by God's own call.

The leader begins, by praying for the person on her or his right hand, after which the person to the leader's left prays for the leader, and so on sequentially around the circle. Members may choose to pray silently, rather than aloud, when their turn comes, but it is helpful to the group process if they announce that intention and then say Amen when they are finished so that the next person knows when to begin. When the prayers are finished, there is a moment of silence before the group adjourns.

EXAMPLE

Sharon says "Let's take a time of prayer now, can we?, offering up to our God all the important things that have surfaced in our hearts and minds in the last few minutes. We are all praying for each other, of course, but each of us will be formally responsible to pray for one other—the person on our right hand—on behalf of the whole group. Our prayer is that each of us may be enabled in what we feel we have been invited to do or be. I'll begin.

"Our God, I thank you for our brother Bill and his great energy. I thank you that he is asking what it is he really wants, and I pray that you will help him be discerning as he goes about those tasks he is responsible for in the next week. Amen." The group repeats Amen.

Mary prays, "Father/Mother God, you have blessed Sharon with your gentleness; give her now strength to face unknown situations in the power of your Spirit. Amen." All repeat Amen.

Ann whispers, "Lord, be good to Mary. Amen." All repeat Amen.

Charles says, "I'll pray silently." He does so for a few moments, taking Ann's hand in his as he prays. He says, "Amen," and all repeat it, including Ann.

Jim prays, "Lord Jesus Christ, you provide the model for us of a righteous life; you alone are holy; you are our judge and our savior. Your teachings are full of wisdom, and I pray you'll show Charles how to be wise too. In your holy name I pray. Amen." All repeat Amen.

Bill prays, "Father, I offer my friend Jim to you. You know better than I all the desires of his heart, but I pray that you will help him to follow your lead. Amen." All repeat Amen.

There is a moment of companionable silence, and then a couple of people begin to stretch and others softly to talk. Several of them walk over and hug Ann. Gradually, they all head for the kitchen to set out dinner.

Summary

That is all there is to the group lectio process (for your reference, it is summarized in chart 1). Lectio has both the simplicity of the gospel and the implicit challenge the gospel holds to make it a vital reality in every person's life.

You may be tempted to elaborate on this basic framework, but it is best to stay simple since lectio's great power is found in its ability to balance elements of activity and receptivity and use silence as a gentle and unhurried way to open each human heart to God's Word, already active therein. May you be blessed by its practice!

CHART 1

The Process of Group Lectio

The process of group lectio can be summarized as follows:

Prepare.

Take a moment to come fully into the present. Sit comfortably alert, eyes closed, and center yourself with breathing.

1. Hear the word (that is addressed to you).

First reading (twice). Listen for the word or phrase that attracts from the passage. Repeat it over to yourself softly during a one-minute silence. When the leader gives the signal, say aloud *only* that word or phrase (no elaboration).

2. Ask "How is my life touched?" (by this word).

Second reading. Listen to discover how your life is touched today by this passage. Consider possibilities or receive a sensory impression during the two minutes of silence. When the leader gives the signal, speak a sentence or two beginning with "I hear," "I see," "I sense" (or you may pass).

3. Ask, "Is there an invitation here?" (for you).

Third reading. Listen to discover a possible invitation relevant to the next few days. Ponder it during several minutes of silence. When the leader gives the signal, speak of your sense of invitation (or you may pass).

4. Pray (for one another to be enabled to respond).

Pray, aloud or silently, for God to help the person on your right respond to the invitation received.

After this process, the group may share how it went, if desired.

CHAPTER 2

The Heart and Rhythm of Lectio Practice

This chapter, on the heart and rhythm of lectio practice, is intended to help groups understand and value the foundational structure of group lectio. This structure, though loose-fitting, has been molded over the centuries as a guide to being open to Christ's Spirit. The heart and rhythm of lectio's structure centers in a balance of elements essential to our humanness:

- The material and spiritual realms
- Activity and receptivity
- Word and silence
- Community life supporting individuals

Balance is the key to these elements. The heart and rhythm of lectio involves continuing, organic interchange and counterpoint between the various elements crucial to our wholeness as humans. If we are not particularly attentive to this balance, we may be practicing lectio without its heart!

The implicit structure of lectio is revealed in this chapter through exploration of these four balanced elements at lectio's center, its heart and rhythm. Attentiveness to this heart and rhythm allows deeper encounter with the living God. However, lectio's structure is somewhat foreign to modern life-styles, so we usually find it necessary to discipline ourselves in order to stay attentive to its heart and rhythm. The remainder of this chapter gives the theoretical basis for lectio's balanced structure, corresponding to the four elements set forth above, combined with specific examples of our imaginary group to demonstrate lectio at work.

The "bottom line" implicit in all that follows can be described in terms of certain practical behaviors essential for fidelity to the heart and rhythm of lectio. These practical behaviors do not correspond directly to the theoretical balances explored in the rest of the chapter but they are implicit in all of them. Therefore, it may be useful to set them out here at the beginning. They are as follows:

- Stay with the words of the passage.
  (Don't theologize or generalize.)
- Stay with the outline of the process.
  (Don't elaborate or skip any parts.)
- Take time to prepare and to close every session.
  (Consent to be here, not somewhere else.)
- Stay open to the unknown. (Watch with awe.)

Balance and behavior are integrated in lectio's heart and rhythm. Let's explore this further.

The Material and Spiritual Realms

Lectio is founded in a Christian theology that takes the principle of incarnation quite seriously, not only as it applies to God's work and life, but also as it expresses a basic truth about *human* life: We are invited to share in the divine life, even as we go about our everyday activities! Incarnation is expressed vividly in the Hebrew Scriptures at the moment of creation, when God breathes spirit into dust:

> Then the Lord God formed man from dust of the ground, and breathed into his nostrils the breath of life; and the man became a living being. (Gen. 2:7–8)

Incarnation takes its highest form in the New Testament, when Christ is born as son of God and son of man:

> The Holy Spirit will come upon you [Mary], and the power of the Most High will overshadow you; therefore the child to be born will be holy; he will be called the Son of God. (Luke 1:35)

And yet this gift of Christ, god and human, is intended to include rather than exclude us. We are invited to share in the divine life! This is a central message of God's action in creation and in Christ's birth. It is almost too much to take in! It means that our own wholeness requires nurture of the twin aspects of our being, divine and human, spirit and body.

Lectio is specifically designed to help us do this, as it engages both our active abilities (expressing our human material form) and our receptive abilities (expressing our need for the divine spirit or inspiration). Lectio turns rhythmically to the one and then the other, in an oscillation very similar to that of heartbeat or breath, where material and spiritual are essential elements of a unified process.

Before we can effectively practice balance of material and spiritual realms in our lectio, we need first to acknowledge that the principle of incarnation is not well modeled in our culture. At one extreme, our cultural outlook is materialistic; we are fundamentally skeptical of any experience that cannot be measured and verified by everyone else. We often assume that only the "sensible" exists. As a result, we need both practice and support to trust our lectio experiences of God when they transcend the senses.

The recent "New Age" alternative approach to contemporary living basically goes to the other extreme, emphasizing spiritual realities by displacing material ones. This outlook presumes that the visible or bodily (that is, the normal struggles of daily life) is illusory, and that people only suffer because they allow themselves to get stuck in unreal appearances. As a result, we may feel guilty and somehow "unspiritual" if we are in pain or feel grief.

Both these cultural portraits are caricatures, of course, but each is faithful to the implicit and powerful message of our culture: that the nuts and bolts of daily life bear *no* relationship to a spiritual journey, and that if there is anything "real" to be gained through spiritual growth, it will only be in some distant and amorphous twilight zone. The insistent message is that there is no authentic transforming spiritual power in the midst of material life.

Lectio invariably tests us in this arena, because it weaves a way through life that insists on balance and integration of the material and the spiritual. Although it involves contemplation, or resting in the wordless experience of God, it also involves mission, or being sent from the embrace of God to the embrace of actual life experiences to discover how God is also present there. The experience of lectio is involvement in a flow back and forth between the material and the spiritual, which creates new possibilities in the here and now, manifesting the inherent union of spiritual and material realms. Thus lectio directly challenges the dominant world view in which we live.

The problem for us Christians is that when we take the fullness of our faith seriously, seeking not to deny either the material or the spiritual dimensions of our actual experience, we are going into uncharted waters. We are behaving "oddly"—somewhat like sailing out across the seas when "everyone knows" that the earth is flat! To rely on God and follow God's daily guidance is hard work and requires great discipline and willingness to learn. Lectio invites us to do just that, and gives us the means to practice it, for it is based in an intimacy of life experience and the gifts of God.

The following example shows how the tendency to expect life experience to be purely physical or purely spiritual can interfere with effective lectio.

EXAMPLE

The group of six is meeting this time (a month later) at Jim and Ann's home. On the drive over, Charles says to Sharon, "You know, I really don't get this lectio business. We're supposed to start by listening for a word of God, but frankly, I don't know what God sounds like! Isn't this whole process a little like self-hypnosis?"

Sharon nods, "It does seem like kind of a leap in the dark to act as if God really wants to speak to me about my ordinary life issues. But when I just give myself to the process, something happens. Usually "God's voice" sounds very much like my own, but the insights I get are so practical and so freeing that I'm glad to stay with it!"

"Is it important that I pay attention to these reservations of mine," Charles asks, "or do you think I should just forget them and plunge in?"

"Maybe both!" she replies, "It seems important that each of us be clear about where we really are on this, and not to force something artificial. But for me, there's such a yearning inside; I *need* something more than already exists in my life. I want more, and I don't know how to get it, except by trying out a process I have reason to trust, and watching what happens."

Charles grins ruefully, "Yeah, Sharon, who knows but what God can work even through self-hypnosis. I'll hang in there a while!"

Meanwhile at the house, Mary and Bill have arrived early, and Ann and Mary are upstairs with the children. Ann confesses, "I find this lectio process so different than my usual way of prayer that I hardly know what to make of it. For the last year I've been practicing a form of meditation where I have learned to clear my mind of all thoughts, so it seems somehow wrong just to *let* thoughts come in. And when they're about the problems in my life, I feel like I lose my peace completely. All prayer just leaves me."

Mary sympathizes, "Oh, that must be so troubling!" She is distracted for a moment by her youngest child, and then she turns back to Ann. "I wonder if maybe prayer has a bigger range than we have imagined before? Maybe it includes both that deep inner peace you've found *and* something that seems more like inner disturbance but is really a way of opening the tough issues of our lives directly to God? What do you think?"

Ann says, "Well, maybe. I guess it's worth a try. But it's real hard for me."

In this example, Charles represents the "materialist" view—that a thing needs to be tangible in order to be "real." Ann represents the "spiritualist" view—that we are really only in the presence of God when we are feeling calm and somewhat remote from practical problems. In both cases, it is helpful for them to realize the assumptions they bring to lectio, because if we don't know where we are, we can never find our way home. Always we begin with both acceptance of what is *and* a willingness not to be confined by it. The group and the individual start with respect for present dispositions and encourage gentle openness to discover what actually is present and possible.

Internal disquiet caused by seeing the world's viewpoint alongside the biblical one, in relation to oneself, is often a sign of genuine desire to transcend cultural limits. It is not necessarily negative, and need not be stopped or "fixed" as soon as possible. Inner disquiet may be the way in which we grow beyond our assumptions or express our hope for possibilities we cannot even imagine. A supportive group that accepts, with love, a wide range of experience and biases provides a wonderfully free environment, one where members can test their fragile longings for fullness of life. New life comes in the practice of patience and gentleness—even with oneself—not in argument or harangue or acting as we think we should.

Activity and Receptivity

In lectio, we are seeking to be transformed into Christ. That transformation is gradual and grounded in daily life experiences, so it is often invisible to us while it is happening. It is only afterward that we can look back to observe how much change God has worked in us. This ongoing, mostly invisible work of lectio is called *formation*, meaning the kind of slow but precise shaping of clay by a potter. Yet the image of a potter is not quite apt, because God does not move to shape without the willingness of we clay lumps. Lectio involves a balance of activity and receptivity: we actively seek God's hand, we are receptive to gradual shaping. We are conscious and cooperative clay, engaging our will with God's in a process of spiritual formation.

It is not easy for us to distinguish between "will" and "willingness," and this theological language is often difficult for us. The Hebrew Scriptures avoided our difficulty by speaking of the *heart* as the locus of the active-receptive relationship with God in spiritual formation. For them, the heart involved not just activity but also receptivity. The heart was seen as the inner seat of the human's whole being. As such, it was the organ of capacity for God's very self. As such, it was the locus not only of choice and motive, but also of one's fundamental orientation toward life. In the heart, we are formed and reformed into the person we most long to be. So the psalmist cries out his deep desire for personal transformation in these simple words:

> [O God,] give me understanding, that I may keep your law and observe it with my whole heart. (Ps. 119:34)

When we consider this place in ourselves that is designed for active receptiveness to God, the place that gradually expresses and develops our unique wholeness, we realize much of its work is hidden from us. It is at the center of our being, yet out of sight, the physical reality of the human heart revealing a spiritual truth. Its minute-by-minute rhythmic motion is foundational for our very life, yet ultimately mysterious. Our spiritual heart, like our physical heart, is aided by our supportive actions (regular exercise, sound diet, and so forth), but it is not finally under our control.

Oddly, we express and cooperate with (or resist) this God-receptive, active center of the heart primarily in very practical and "unimportant" ways: in the routine decisions of each day, in the motives we utilize and the desires we pursue, in the development of those habits of speech and action which cumulatively form our temperament and disposition. Our capacity for God is developed most directly not so much by our intellect, nor by our emotions, as by our habits and predispositions to action, our choices and our wishes.

Lectio's structure is designed to form this essential center of our being, which is our capacity for God, our disposition to act, our heart and will. Lectio asks that we lay our life issues alongside the patterns described in Scripture, finding there a template that helps us be who we are fully meant to be. Lectio takes both thought and emotion, and balances them intentionally in relationship to our capacity for God. Spiritual growth is fulfilled in the union of our will with God's; lectio enlarges the heart, which is the capacity for such union. The model of such growth is Christ, whose will was so attuned to the Father's that both Persons mutually abide in each other.

A life lived from the heart, with activity and receptivity in balance, is not common in our culture. It definitely is a risk to undertake the work of the heart with God. Yet lectio promises the fruitfulness of this risk, inviting us to live to the full.

The group example that follows is intended to suggest how lectio encourages formation through a balance of activity and receptivity, while waiting until people are ready. The basic lectio structure allows the essential mix of action and control, receptivity and release to be practiced safely and in good time. Lectio's reflective structure allows each person gradually to test life experience from the heart, that is, in accordance with God's will.

The balance of activity and receptivity especially requires the foundational lectio behaviors mentioned at the beginning of this chapter. The heart is truly formed in the basic structure of lectio; it is the hidden heart at which this structure is aimed. So as you review this group example, keep in mind these structural behaviors expressing commitment to enlarging your heart for God:

- Stay with the words of the passage.
  (Don't theologize or generalize.)
- Stay with the outline of the process.
  (Don't elaborate or skip any parts.)
- Take time to prepare and to close every session.
  (Consent to be here, and not somewhere else.)
- Stay open to the unknown. (Watch with awe.)

EXAMPLE

The group has gathered in Jim and Ann's living room. Mary is tonight's leader. She has begun to review the basic format of lectio when Charles interrupts. "Oh, Mary, we know the rules! Let's just move on to the Scripture!" Mary looks annoyed, but begins immediately to read the passage for tonight, Mark 1:35–37:

> In the morning, while it was still very dark, [Jesus] got up and went out to a deserted place, and there he prayed. And Simon and his companions hunted for him. When they found him, they said to him, "Everyone is searching for you!"

As soon as Mary finishes reading the first time, Charles says, "everyone." Bill says, "in the morning." Ann says, "prayed." Jim says, "very dark." Sharon says, "hunted." And Mary says, "a deserted place."

Then Mary says, "I think I was supposed to read the passage again and then we were supposed to have a time of silent listening before we shared anything. So this next time, please wait until I give the signal before you say anything." She asks Charles to read the passage the second time.

There is silence after the reading until Mary says, "Okay, now please briefly share, if you wish, about how this passage seems to touch your life today."

Jim says, "Dark was my word, and I'm really in the dark about this process. I don't see how this nonsense is supposed to get us in touch with God at all!"

Ann says, "Maybe we should take time now to talk with Jim about his concern?" But Mary quickly responds, "Let's go ahead with our process as planned, and then save a little time at the end for all of us to talk about how it's going for us generally. Okay?" There are a few nods, and then some more silence.

The group continues with the process, sharing how they feel touched, hearing the reading a third time, silently listening until the signal, then each sharing any sense of invitation. Finally each prays for the person on the right. They close with the Lord's Prayer.

Mary says, "Before we get up, let's take a few minutes to talk together about the process of lectio. How is it going for us?"

Jim says, "Well, I find I'm kind of fighting it because it is so unlike my previous experience with the Bible, and I miss thinking about things in a systematic way. But I was really taken by surprise in the middle of our session tonight. At first I was irritated that you didn't stop and talk about what was bothering me. But then as we continued to be together here with the Scripture and the companionable silence, a mantle of peace just seemed to drop down over my shoulders, almost as if God were putting his arm around me. I still feel in the dark—I didn't get any ideas at all—but suddenly it occurred to me that God may be more than all my ideas about him. The peace I felt was so real! I guess what I really need to do is just stay with this stuff long enough to give it a fair try."

Charles says, "Yeah, Jim, I was talking with Sharon about my discomfort just before the meeting. This lectio stuff is real different, but also very moving for me. I still don't know whether I'm making it all up in my own mind, or what, but I'd like to keep with it for . . . what, maybe six months, before I decide. . . . By the way, Mary, I realize I was really out of line trying to move you along quickly tonight. I think maybe hearing those instructions each time actually helps me simmer down and get present and relaxed, open to whatever will happen here."

Mary replies, "Thanks, Charles. It's not easy to be leader, or know exactly what is important about this procedure. And it's very difficult for me not to jump in when I sense someone is hurting, as I was concerned Jim might be tonight. I've wondered if the formal structure might prevent us from offering each other the support that we came for. But tonight, as I kept us with the format, I somehow felt that the lectio process itself gave me an important *new* way to give support, and to get it."

Sharon adds, "I think we all feel some comfort and some discomfort with lectio. But I'm also sensing that we don't think we will really get what it offers until we've tried it for a while."

Ann says, "I'm also have some difficulty with lectio. It's not easy for me to let words and images from my life come into my prayer time. I get all jangled, and I feel as if I've lost God. But I realize that when we finish lectio, I feel just as centered as I do in my meditative prayer, and I really appreciate having some people to share the journey with me. So I'm glad we're doing it."

The lectio process has an integrity of its own, related to its objective of enlarging the heart for God through balance of action and reception. This means it may raise mild discomfort of various sorts, but also that it is amenable to a fair test. Stay with it, and be attentive to what is happening. Continually return to the basic directions, and remain as close to them as possible, but don't set them in concrete. Remember that the objective is formation in God's Spirit, and lectio is intended to increase our receptivity to that Spirit.

Word and Silence

The third element of lectio's heart and rhythm is balance of word and silence. Lectio's structure powerfully balances both word and silence. It is rooted in word: It begins with the word of Scripture and seeks the Word as Son. It is continuously interacting with the "word" of our personal lives, that is, with our thoughts and dreams, fears, worries, and delights.

> In the beginning was the Word, and the Word was with God and the Word was God. . . . What has come into being in him was life, and the life was the light of all people. (John 1:1, 3b–4)

Lectio is also rooted in silence. We prepare for lectio by letting outer and inner noise be released. We start and end lectio with rest in God, receiving without comment whatever is given. We seek only to speak those actual words in lectio sharing that are born out of our silent pondering while enfolded in God's life.

> I wait for the Lord, my soul waits, and in his word I hope; my soul waits for the Lord more than those who watch for the morning, more than those who watch for the morning. (Ps. 130:5–6)

The balance of word and silence is incredibly difficult for us to sustain because our culture is so oriented toward word and so ignorant of silence. Wherever we go, we are bombarded with noise: shopping malls, offices, elevators, on the telephone, in the car—everywhere! Most of us have little or no experience of silence, and we may find it disturbing or alien. One minute of silence in a public meeting, even at church, seems intolerably long. We seem to think that silence is the absence of something, and our nature abhors a vacuum. Yet we might wonder whether our near-frantic efforts to be surrounded by noise suggest a deeper fear—that silence is the presence of something so powerful that it is to be feared.

Yet silence is essential for listening. How awkward it is to try to have a serious conversation with someone wearing earphones! How hard to communicate a message to someone wielding a leaf blower! How impossible to reach someone absorbed in a television program! In any relationship there must be listening for there to be communication, and that is no less true of our relationship with God than of any other.

With God, we speak our needs, our longings, our hungers, our pain, our hope. And then we listen, because we speak all these things in the hope of being *heard* by God. We speak because we need something we cannot supply ourselves. We speak because we long for new life that is beyond our capacity to bring to our experience, but that we sense, we pray, is possible for us. We pray that somehow the divine can penetrate the earthly in our particular case, that there is something better and different for us just out of our reach. So in prayer, we also listen. We wait. We quiver in expectancy that God will respond to us.

Word in prayer is our self-giving. Silence in prayer is receptivity to the self-giving of God. The balance of the two creates possibilities beyond our imagining! Lectio is rooted in this formative balance of word and silence.

EXAMPLE

Our group of six has now met over several months, and they are beginning to be more relaxed with the process. Tonight they are at Bill and Mary's home, and Jim is leading. They have just heard the first double reading of the passage:

> Treasure up my commandments within you, making your ear attentive to wisdom and inclining your heart to understanding. . . . [C]ry out for insight. (Prov. 2:1a–3a)

There is a minute of silence, and Jim invites people to share the word that came to them. Charles says, "salvation."

There is a moment's silence, and then Jim asks, "Is there a direct word from the passage itself that you also heard, Charles?"

He looks up, surprised, and after a moment says, "uh, treasure."

Sharon says, "incline." Ann says, "inclining your heart." Bill says "understanding." And Mary says, "cry out." Jim says, "commandments."

Mary reads the passage a second time, and Jim asks people to listen in the silence for the way the passage touches their lives. After about twenty seconds, Ann blurts out, "I'm trying to figure out how the heart can be inclined. Does that mean it is turned on its side, or turned around, or at an angle, or what? And if the heart is not in the right inclination, does it mess up the other internal organs, I mean, would there be a lung problem or something like that? Sometimes I really have trouble breathing. . . ."

Jim touches Ann's hand and says, "Let's just take a bit more time in the silence, and see what it tells us." Ann blushes, and subsides into silence.

When Jim invites sharing, about a minute later, Charles says, "I thought of going to heaven and finding a big pile of gold there just for me. Is salvation like a big pile of gold? Surely not! But what does salvation mean? What is treasure? It's confusing."

Ann passes, and Bill says, "Well, I got the picture of a mathematical equation representing understanding. I realize that doesn't offhand seem to make much sense, but I think it probably comes from my extensive analytical training, because equations stand for the means by which we come to understanding. . . ." Jim says, "Thanks, Bill."

All three of these responses are ways of overbalancing lectio in favor of word. Charles picked a concept to interpret the Scripture (salvation), instead of a word from the Scripture itself. Ann jumped in before the leader gave the signal, anxious to pour out whatever was beginning to emerge before it had time to grow into fullness in the silence. And Bill felt compelled to explain or rationalize why he had received the image that came. There are places for all of these responses, but lectio is not that place. There are times for activity and responsibility, but lectio is designed to help us gain access to those *new* resources beyond ourself, available only in receptivity. In lectio, we are seeking that transformation into Christ which comes as gift to those who wait in need and longing. In lectio, we let a new and powerful word be born in the soil of silence, by following the common procedures that facilitate this balance.

And, of course, there can be imbalance toward silence as well as imbalance toward word.

EXAMPLE

The remaining group members take their turns at sharing after the second reading. Jim says, "I'm in such a peaceful, imageless place that I'm finding words intrusive. I pass."

Sharon says, "I sometimes think I would prefer to be in a convent, where I could spend all day turning my ear to wisdom."

And Mary concludes, "When I think of the circumstances of my life, I want to cry out in anger and pain. I would rather not think of them, but just be here in this warm fellowship for a while, forgetting all that other stuff."

These responses tend toward imbalance in the other direction. The desire to "escape" is understandable, and is often healing in small doses, but the goal of lectio is the integration of life and prayer. Lectio intends that we bring to bear in word/activity those inner certainties experienced in silence/rest. In lectio, we seek to experience rest in order to let it inform our daily struggles, decisions, and actions. When we refuse to let the gospel light up our present life situation honestly and lovingly, we are retreating from this essential pole of life's activity, and thus losing a necessary human balance. Our lives are to be changed by our faith; in order for this to happen, we must inquire of our actual life experiences how faith gently informs and empowers them.

The element of silence in lectio brings opportunity to let our few words be genuinely formed from the receptive encounter with God. The element of word acknowledges that in the encounter with God we are empowered and sent to be God's life in the world, while it also helps us to be specific about what that might mean today to us.

Community Life Supporting Individuals

The form of lectio we are using is set within a small Christian community, where we can mutually support each other while we navigate the testing waters of the presence of Christ's living Spirit in our midst. We usually find that when we commit ourselves to spiritual growth, we long for practical support and accountability to others sharing our commitment to Christ. We have a deep desire to be known by others as we really are, that is, as we are known by Christ, celebrating our real strengths and complementing our real weaknesses. We long to talk with others about things that really confuse us, as well as about things that really delight us. There are very few places in our world where we can do this, but an authentic Christian small group is one of them. Thus a small group is an ideal setting, a means of true community life, for the practice of lectio.

However, although small groups seem to be sprouting up all over, they are often a disappointment or of very short duration. A central problem is that our culture tends to be hostile not only to things spiritual but also to things communal. We live and breathe in a setting that exalts individualism and rewards independence. Indeed, we commonly react to words such as *community, commitment,* and *dependence* with wariness, anticipating limits on our freedom. We don't really know how to trust each other, how to support each other in pain, how to disagree in love, how to be genuinely respectful of each other, how to be "for" each other in the long haul. Whereas a lectio group only requires limited commitment over a short term, it does call for us to practice skills that we may not have previously developed—skills that balance community and individual needs.

Lectio creates a bond among group members that truly manifests the body of Christ. The nature of this body is described by St. Paul: "It has many different parts, each individually important, all somehow contributing to the whole" (adapted from 1 Cor. 12:12–27). In Christ, we come to know one another as kin, united in our love and longing for God, however great our diversity. After a few months of practicing lectio, we might find ourselves surprised that, although we may not yet have discovered "basic" things about others in the group (such as how many children they have or what their jobs are), we feel like brothers and sisters in a shared love that has existed forever.

Today we know a great deal about fellowship and psychological needs, but we have remarkably little experience of Christian community, that is, of being the body of Christ. In Christ, we care for one another *in the context* of awareness that God is doing more for each of us than any of us can desire or even imagine! This awareness of God's care does not exempt us from the responsibility of being a caring community, but it does relieve us of that compulsive serving that so often distracts us from our own responsibility to and direct engagement with God. In our gathered community, there is a Spirit at work that is more powerful than any individual care and that is deeply engaged with every single one of us. The community of Christ's body is one in which we know each other through the eyes of Christ, as it were. This is different from our usual way of experiencing each other; there is something radically distinctive about such mutual knowing.

Group lectio allows us to practice together what it is to grow into this balanced community, this body of Christ. The key to balance in Christian community life is this: Whatever is happening in any person at this moment, Christ is now active in it, bringing forth life and giving growth.

Four practices help us make Christ the center of our lectio community life so that our group is actively supporting individuals in their unique spiritual journeys:

- Speaking the truth
- Admitting strong emotions
- Listening in love
- Confidentiality

These four practices, explored in the following sections, are a necessary part of the covenanting and leadership tools discussed in chapter 3.

SPEAKING THE TRUTH

Speaking the truth in love, we must grow up in every way into him who is the head, into Christ, from whom the whole body [is] joined. . . . So then, putting away falsehood, let all of us speak the truth to our neighbors, for we are members of one another. (Eph. 4:15–16a, 25)

In a healthy body, each part must both be itself as fully as possible and aid the other parts to become what they are. Among other things, this means learning to live and speak as much as possible in the truth. For example, if one ankle is badly sprained but pretends it is not, there will nevertheless be additional strain placed on the other leg to compensate, and possibly areas of the back as well. Or we might be strongly right-handed, and the overreliance upon that strength can cause gradual deterioration of left-hand capability. If we imagine parts of the body acting to deceive each other, such that all the affected parts are making difficult adjustments but pretending they are not, we can get some idea of how dishonesty pervades and distorts community life.

Thus, a balanced community life depends in part on our mutual commitment to work toward truthfulness in our relationships with one another and with God. Truthfulness does not mean making ourselves unnecessarily vulnerable, nor does it mean verbally assaulting others. But it does mean speaking without deliberate deception; sharing our own thoughts, feelings, and dreams as fully as we feel able; and mirroring as accurately as possible what we hear from others. Truthfulness means speaking for ourselves and taking responsibility for our own ideas and feelings, as well as being aware and remaining connected through disagreements in love. Unity in diversity is a goal not easily realized, and it helps to recognize that we are working toward it (in the power of the Spirit), rather than inheriting it ready made in our Christian groups.

Lectio groups are a means to seek the Word of God in order to bring it into our lives. God's Word is obviously vibrant, multifaceted, powerful, and often challenging. The goal of lectio is so to incarnate this transforming Word that increasingly we are able to give it forth as our own personal truth. This is a strenuous discipline, but there are a couple of basic ways to practice truth in love in our lectio groups. The first is to speak with "I" messages, that is to express our own feelings, doubts, and desires, rather than talking about what others need or giving advice. The second is not to avoid conflict, but instead welcome it as a means of gaining better perspective of the whole.

EXAMPLE

Our group of six have gathered at the home of Sharon and Charles for a lectio meeting, and have listened for the second time to this reading:

> Above all, clothe yourselves with love, which binds everything together in perfect harmony. And let the peace of Christ rule in your hearts, to which indeed you were called in the one body. And be thankful. Let the word of Christ dwell in you richly. (Col. 3:14–16a)

Tonight Bill is leading, and when he gives the go-ahead to share about how members lives have been touched, Jim begins. "My word is 'perfect harmony,' and I can't help but reflect on how little harmony there is in the church. They bicker all the time about unimportant things, and never set aside time for important things like Bible study. That's why I joined this group, and I think every member of all the churches should join one too!"

Bill asks simply, "Is there something in particular that touches *you* about perfect harmony, Jim?"

Jim exclaims, "Yes, of course, that's what I'm saying. I really miss it!"

Mary says, "My word was 'be thankful,' and my experience of our church is different from Jim's. In the silence I felt myself a part of a circle dance, with so many friends from church holding hands and dancing together with Jesus at the center of the circle. And I am filled with gratitude."

The time of lectio itself is not a time for extended conversation, either about the personal nature of Jim's reactions or about a difference of viewpoints between Jim and Mary. But it is important to be moving toward a deepened ability to speak the truth in love, in all of our exchanges, because that is a primary means by which we become members of Christ's body to each other. In our lectio groups, we have an opportunity to practice what communication might be like when it is genuinely formed by the Word of God.

This kind of communication does not mean constant agreement, nor even lukewarm tolerance, but rather that we commit always to valuing ourselves and others, aware that in some way we are given to each other to be who we really are. In lectio, we practice the root meaning of *benediction: bene* means good or well and *dicere* means to speak. So when we speak well, when we speak the truth in love, we are a source of blessing to each other. We intend the best for each other, as well as for ourselves.

ADMITTING STRONG EMOTIONS

Reflecting on speaking the truth, we realize that it is impossible to speak the truth if we are not living the truth. We can only communicate that which we have allowed to come to consciousness in ourselves. We can only speak about that which we know because we are living it. It is not easy to let the truth about ourselves rise fully into our awareness, for when we do, we often are faced with painful or difficult facts that we cannot change. For instance, we may be painfully lonely or agonizingly helpless. We are not accustomed to admitting feelings that we cannot immediately direct toward a solution. And admission means both willingness to allow something to enter our consciousness and willingness to speak or share. The risk of admission is as old as humankind. Many of the Psalms speak eloquently of this dilemma.

> In the day of my trouble I seek the Lord; in the night my hand is stretched out without wearying; my soul refuses to be comforted. I think of God, and I moan; I meditate and my spirit faints." (Ps. 77:2–3)

As we live honestly into the depths of ourselves before God in group lectio, we may find strong emotions surfacing in us, and we are encouraged at least to admit them to ourselves, as well as to admit them in the safe context of the group when we are ready. Two frequently experienced emotions are sadness and anger.

In the midst of a lectio session, we may find ourselves in tears or pain, awareness of loss and loneliness. We may have an acute sense of incompleteness and inadequacy, or we may admit all that we long for and have not found. It is not surprising that when we experience directly both our need and God's generosity, we receive what the tradition calls "the gift of tears." Yet often these tears are felt to be embarrassing or awkward, not only for the one affected but also for the group. Group members may respond by ignoring or covering over the intense emotion: "It will be all right!" Or perhaps we make an attempted rescue, thinking that, having been offered another's pain, we need to fix it.

Yet being together in Christ usually calls for another response. First we simply hear and acknowledge that one of us is experiencing grief, feelings of limitation, or other pain. And together on behalf of the one who suffers, we offer the wounds to Christ in our midst, knowing that he is already moving toward healing them more fully than we can know. This does not mean that we discard helpful resources we might offer to each other at a later time. It simply means that above all in our lectio group, we are attuned primarily to Christ's powerful presence active with us now as we come together in his name, and that we first turn to him for help.

After acknowledging what is actually occurring, we offer it to Christ among us. We may intensify our silent prayer, attentive to God in our midst and earnestly holding up the one who is in pain to God's all-gracious embrace. We do not know how God may be working in this suffering. The experience of loss or inadequacy may be a necessary prelude to some important conversion of heart; the sense of incompleteness or restlessness may be a necessary prerequisite to a deeper embrace of God. *Every* experience, positive or negative, is just the right thing for us at this moment, if we offer it and ourselves to God's mercy. Group lectio offers a supportive environment in which to believe and *practice* this great mystery of faith. Lectio is a powerful means of mutual support; with it we reveal that our true relationship to each other is *through Christ*.

EXAMPLE

It is now Ann's turn to share after the second reading of Colossians 3:14–16a. She starts to speak, but sobs and swallows several times. Then she gasps for breath and says, "That phrase, 'the peace of Christ,' is like a dagger in my heart. I have so little peace. I do everything wrong; it's so unfair!" Tears stream down her face, and she says no more. Mary slides across the sofa to give Ann a tissue and put an arm around her. There is an uncomfortable silence as Ann continues to cry. The leader, Bill, looks awkward, as if unsure what to do. Gradually Ann's sobs diminish and she quiets in Mary's embrace. Although the silence is somewhat awkward, there is no hurry to end it.

Finally Sharon speaks. "My phrase was 'Christ-dwell.' In some strange way in these last few moments, I have had an acute sense of Christ's presence right here with us, sharing Ann's pain and uniting us all. It was like Mary's dance, but this time a dance of sorrow rather than joy, a gift of being together no matter what." Ann's eyes meet Sharon's and a look of understanding passes between them.

A second strong emotion that may surface in lectio is anger. We may feel that God has abandoned us or that we have been placed in a most unfair situation. We may even experience anger directed at one another, or the group process, because we feel we are not finding what we seek and need from the process. But again, the response of the community in Christ is centered in respect and a certain detachment. Whatever is happening at the moment is in Christ's hands. The anger may simply need to surface so that it can be dealt with in the relationship with God.

The Psalms often express the conviction that God receives our anger willingly; what is crucial is that we persist in the relationship with God, no matter what. The lectio group does not need to accept responsibility for the anger, nor fix it; it needs only to entrust the person and the situation to God, who is present at this moment in the group's midst.

EXAMPLE

Charles now takes his turn sharing. He shifts uncomfortably and says, "The word I got was 'binds,' and right now, I'm feeling pretty tied up. What kind of Christians are we anyway, to sit here helplessly while Ann is feeling such pain? Surely there is something wrong with a process that brings so much junk to the surface. I don't want to be a part of anything that makes people hurt so much!" There is a long, awkward silence.

Jim blurts out, "Aren't we going to respond to Charles?"

Bill shakes his head in confusion and says thoughtfully, "I'm not sure quite what to do now, but if I understand our commitment to each other, the main thing is that we have promised to complete the full lectio format each time, without jumping to anything else during the time itself. And the reason we do that is because we're convinced that somehow Jesus Christ is here with us in a privileged way, especially revealed in the structure of lectio. So, if Ann feels okay about it, I propose that we continue, and then talk more after we are finished, as we need to."

Ann nods, and Bill continues. "My word was also 'peace of Christ,' and a funny image seemed to come to me during the quiet time. What I got was a sense of about ten kids, all bundled up and playing out in the snow. They were laughing and throwing snowballs and crying and shoving and touching and making lots of noise. And yet—maybe it was the softness of the snow, I don't know—but there was overall the strongest sense of peacefulness and rightness and gladness. It was really a kind of celebration, even though it was nothing like I would normally consider as peace. . . .

"Let's go on now to hear the Scripture again, pondering if there is an invitation there for each one of us right now."

Admitting strong emotions is not an easy discipline, and it is likely that the group will experience some discomfort in doing so. But it is also the case that the admission and *offering* to Christ here and now expresses a powerful mode of healing that is generally inaccessible to us if we follow our usual pattern of turning to our own resources at once, rather than waiting in trust for the Spirit.

LISTENING IN LOVE

And [Jesus] said, "Let anyone with ears to hear, listen!" (Mark 4:9)

Community life in Christ is based on good listening. One of our most fundamental needs as human beings is to be listened to and understood. Curiously enough, we do not often experience this. We are more prone to analyze, defend, or attempt to solve the problem, rather than simply hearing and acknowledging one another. Carl Rogers has said, "When I have been listened to and *when I have been heard*, I am able to re-perceive my world in a new way, and to go on."[1]

Authentic listening is a very creative process. None of us really knows ourselves in God until we have been able to speak and be heard at the level of our spirit. Others mirror back to us what we seldom fully understand alone—the particular reality of each human life hidden within Christ in God (Col. 3:3). In true listening, we enable each other to discover and affirm this truth about ourselves. We listen to each other's visions and affirm to each other that we are made to become what we behold.

However, it is difficult to begin speaking of these truths. We try to share an aspect of ourselves that seems incredibly personal and precious, and we are inevitably tentative as we touch the sensitive edges of these realities. At this level, we notice the slightest nuances of response; any boredom, judgment, or disapproval may close us up again for a long time. To give another the gift of listening is to offer a space of real safety and support in which each of us can become the one we are meant to be. And so, in group lectio we begin listening to each other as persons, long before the words can even be formed to express that which is being heard.

We need Christ's help in order to be this kind of listener. Each of us invariably carries biases, prejudices, and other limitations that keep us from being good listeners. Consequently, an important start to the skill of good listening is self-knowledge, so that we can be extra careful in areas where we know we find it difficult to hear. And we need always to be praying that God will enable us to be more open. So listening begins with self-understanding and prayer. And we can supplement these basics with a practical approach.

The main "secret" of good listening is to hear what has actually been said, and to communicate that we have heard it. In listening, we are not trying to form or express our own opinion, to persuade another, or to disprove or defend anything. Rather, we are attentive to what the other is communicating, by word and gesture and personal meaning.

For example, if a married couple is talking with each other, and one says to the other, "I wish you would . . . ," it is a rare spouse who will actually *listen* to the end of the sentence. To listen is to be able to describe in one's own words what it is that the other person is actually saying. Instead, the listener has usually jumped far ahead, either to solve the other's "problem" or defend against a perceived accusation. We often seem to believe that if we let the other person know that we *understand* what he or she has said, we have somehow bound ourselves to *agreeing*. But in fact, what each of us really desires in conversation is simply to be *heard*. Receiving what we wish may be far less important to us than knowing we have been fully heard.

The main way we express good listening skills in lectio is by our prayer at the end, since in general we do not give verbal feedback to one another during the sharing itself. It is also possible to offer one another a brief word of affirmation along with a touch after the session, emphasizing what we heard, rather than any advice we might have. (The section "Covenanting Together," in chapter 3, supplements this discussion on the gift of authentic listening.)

EXAMPLE

In the same group lectio session on Colossians, it is now time for the third period of sharing. Bill asks the group to share now any invitation they have received, and afterwards for each to pray for the person on their right.

Mary begins. "I feel an invitation to be sure that each day includes a few moments of celebrating the good things of that day, sort of to make thankfulness more a regular part of my conscious thought."

Ann says quietly, "There is much in my life that is unpeaceful, but also much that is peaceful. Tonight I have experienced so strongly the love and support of each of you, and that means so much. I feel my invitation is to know that, whatever else is going on, I also have *this* place of refuge and care. I'm so grateful to all of you."

Charles says, "I think the invitation to me is not to run away when feelings get strong, but to accept that Christ can be present in the pain and anger, as much as—or maybe even more than—in joy and peace."

Sharon says, "For me the invitation is to be as tender toward my own pain and sorrow as I can be toward the pain of someone I love."

Jim says, "I feel urged to do something to bring better Bible study to the church."

Bill concludes, "I feel invited to explore more how peace can be found in playfulness." He pauses briefly. "Now let's pray for each other, silently if we wish, but being sure to say 'Amen' when we are finished. . . . God, I pray for Jim, that you will help him to share his gift for Bible study with others, and to discover there the unity in you for which he longs. Amen."

Mary prays, "Father/Mother God, you have given Bill a wonderful vision of play as an expression of your very life. Help him find time and energy to play, both as a means of joy and as a way of union with you. Amen."

Ann prays, "Father, I'm so glad you have given Mary her wonderful capacity to be thankful. Help it grow in her."

Charles prays, "Jesus, I'm grateful that you have shown me Ann's courage tonight, her courage to face pain without running away. I'm glad, too, that you have helped her receive the love we all have for her, and I pray that you will continue to do that every day this week. Amen."

Sharon prays, "Holy Spirit, your ways are often different from ours. Thank you for giving Charles the awareness that you don't leave us but are willing to wrestle with us through *all* thoughts and feelings. Amen."

Jim prays, "Christ our Lord, you shared our sorrow in your passion and death, that we might share your resurrection. I pray especially that you will help Sharon be gentle and accepting of her sorrowing, knowing that you share it with her. Amen."

After a moment, Bill asks, "Do we feel that we want to talk now for a while about tonight's experience?"

Jim says, "I think Charles and Ann should have a chance to say something."

Charles responds, "In the last silence I realized that it wasn't so much what was happening with Ann that upset me, as that her evident pain made me aware of my own. And I wanted to run away. But, as I suggested in my prayer, when I stayed here in the silence, I began to be aware not only of Ann's pain, but of her courage. I realized that if she didn't need to run away or to cover it over, neither did I. She really taught me something very important, and I think I understand lectio better, too."

Ann says, "That's kind of you, Charles, although I don't know that I'm aware of having much courage. But I learned something tonight too. Mary's touch, and the kind of acceptance all of you expressed for my tears, helped me feel that what was happening with me was somehow 'okay,' and certainly in God's hands. Oddly enough, the fact that we continued with our lectio told me that you had confidence that God *is* here embracing me, and I knew I could believe that too."

Bill says, "It seems that it would be good to sum up all our prayers and our discussion with the Lord's Prayer, before we adjourn." And they do so.

There is a kind of humility in being a good active listener. We consent to say what seems obvious in order to let others know that we really care about what they are saying. When we state in our own words what others have communicated, it is usually received as a powerful affirmation. It may seem that this "repetition" contributes nothing, but in practice it helps the speaker to feel both known and accepted. Good listening immeasurably helps to build dynamic and trusting group relationships and to strengthen individual growth in Christ.

And, of course, careful listening to one another is a way of being attentive to God. In group lectio, we have gathered to hear the Word of God. We hear this Word in the Scripture, and we listen attentively to help each other hear it in our own lives. Another sensitive listener is the best aid to help us hear the Spirit at work in us, as participants in spiritual direction have known for centuries. Indeed, in many ways, a good group lectio experience is in fact an experience of group spiritual direction.

Let those who have ears, listen!

CONFIDENTIALITY

Lectio is an intimate process. Even when we limit our verbal sharing to a few brief words in the lectio process, we find that we are revealing precious and vulnerable parts of ourselves, for our listening to the combination of Scripture and Spirit touches chords of our deepest desires as human beings.

Intimacy at this level is risky, involving not only our longing for transformation but also our inevitable recognition of the most broken and least "acceptable" parts of ourselves. We may fear that others will not treat these sacred parts of ourselves tenderly, or we may not have language to express our new awareness. For us today, it is easier to talk about money, perhaps even about sex, than it is to talk about a vital relationship with God. When we share our spiritual life with others, we are known by each other in a profoundly intimate way, and both courage and mutual respect are required to sustain this depth of community life. Each session's leader and all the other group members share responsibility for maintaining these safe boundaries of courage and mutual respect. Chapter 3 gives more insight on this aspect of the leader's role.

Intimacy cannot and should not be demanded, and it is well for participants to be somewhat cautious at first, taking time to let authentic trust build in the group. Nothing requires that we "bare all" in the first meeting, and prudence suggests that everyone honor a gradual and organic pace in the development of deep mutuality.

Sharing is never to be forced. Everyone should be permitted to pass, at any point, for any reason or no reason. Often people pass either because they have not yet heard anything (or what they have heard has not yet formed into words) or because what they have heard is so intimate, so powerful, and perhaps so painful, that they are not yet able to speak it. Whatever the reason, the decision to remain silent is best met with respect and gentleness. Each person knows for him- or herself when sharing is premature and when it is safe. It is vital to group life and individual growth to honor this reticence.

[Jesus said:] In everything do to others as you would have them do to you. (Matt. 7:12a)

Above all, confidentiality is essential. Whatever is shared in the group should never be spoken of outside the group unless it is by the person who shared it. A spouse not present should not be told; members not present that week should not be told what a third party shared, although of course anyone may speak of what they themselves said. In general, it is better that group members should not speak among themselves about anyone else's sharing or their situations as revealed in previous meetings. We never know how our "innocent" conversation may connect with what others know to create a misleading impression or negative effect.

Yet confidentiality is easier asked for than achieved. We have very little practice with it, seeming almost to feel we have an obligation to tell whatever we know! We may tell ourselves that we speak about another's situation out of concern for them—and that is often true—but we can inadvertently do serious harm by speaking out, even about something that seems to be minor. However, confidentiality is a genuine prerequisite to the vulnerability sharing in lectio, and is thus an essential part of the group's commitment to each other. Confidentiality enables us to risk faith-sharing with one another, to risk speaking with one another about how we sense God is moving in our lives.

The practices of prudence, respect for reticence, and confidentiality do not eliminate the need for courage in sharing. There will continue to be risk in expressing to others about the inner dynamics of faith. As we begin to notice and articulate the inner yearnings that express our deepest essence, we are as vulnerable as a newborn child. And we need as much emotional tenderness and care from those with whom we share as does a baby. But in a safe setting, such sharing can truly be life-giving, for together we are best able to affirm and embrace the unique self that is truly our own in Christ.

EXAMPLE

Our group of six is meeting again, this time at Jim and Ann's home, with Jim leading the session. The Scripture is Isaiah 42:3:

> A bruised reed he will not break, and a dimly burning wick he will not quench; he will faithfully bring forth justice.

The group has heard the final reading and is sharing whatever invitation the passage seems to hold for them today.

Bill says, "I feel invited to express my thanks for this group. In the past, I have been in groups where something I said in confidence came back to me later in a very public forum. I'm really grateful that this has been a place where I can explore my ambivalence about my job without fearing that I'll hear about it from my boss in a few weeks. I'm not sure that I really would want to leave my job, but I have needed a free space in which to talk about it openly and let off some steam. I feel like I've been a bruised reed, and not only have you been careful not to break me, you are gradually helping the bruises to heal! You've really been there for me, and I'm very thankful."

Sharon says, "I, too, have often felt like a bruised reed. I'm dealing with so many things in my therapy right now, and I really haven't needed to bring up all the details here, but I've needed a safe place to practice being who I am. I'm appreciative that no one has forced me to share when I needed to pass and no one has insisted that I tell more at any moment that I'm able to. I've felt quite free to share all that I wanted to precisely because no one has ever demanded that I share too much! Right now, I think the invitation to me is to recognize the safe places in my life and to risk revealing even more of myself there. I know you have helped me be willing to consider that."

Sharing continues, and the session closes in prayer.

As we have explored these practical aspects of community life as the body of Christ, lectio begins to come to life. We practice being Christ's body through speaking the truth, admitting strong emotions, listening in love, and practicing confidentiality. These practices open us to a way of being together that is radically unlike that generally available in our culture, but close to that promised in Scripture itself and matched by the longings of our hearts.

As Christians, we are promised a oneness in Christ that also empowers the uniqueness of each person. As we come together in love and truth within the body of Christ that we are, our spiritual growth unfolds naturally, as individuals and as community. As we allow ourselves to be known by others as we really are, we also discover more about ourselves as we are known by Christ. As we mutually receive the fullness of individual expression, we come to know what it is to belong to a loving and supportive community. This balance, the experience of community that also supports and strengthens individuals, is a crucial one for effective lectio.

Summary

In this chapter we have revealed the implicit structure of lectio which is often in contrast with the general cultural environment we live in. The positive elements built into the structure of lectio help keep us centered in the process of spiritual growth we intend. These positive elements are all facets of balance, means of integrating important aspects of our human wholeness. They include integration of the material and spiritual realms, of activity and receptivity, of word and silence, and of community life supporting individuals.

Lectio provides a gentle oscillation between review of the situations of our actual daily life and an offering of them to God, which is a way of setting side by side the material and spiritual dimensions of ourselves in order to facilitate their integration. We are seeking transformation into Christ, through the training of our heart for responsiveness to God in the midst of our lives—a blend of action and receptiveness. We sense a need for self-giving as well as for openness to receive the self-giving of God. This rhythm is best facilitated by a mix of word and silence. And we find that, although it is hard work, we are much enriched by practicing all this in a small Christian community. The structure of group lectio offers a firm yet flexible process that gives genuine support for practical and personal spiritual growth.

In lectio, we are growing into the possibilities of transformation in our lives. We are being formed into Christ, together as Christ's body, in order to become open to the new life that is always waiting to emerge where death seems to have triumphed. What a challenge! What an adventure! What an opportunity!

CHAPTER 3

The Basic Tools of Group Lectio Practice

This chapter sets forth practical matters integral to a sound group lectio process. It supplies basic supplementary detail on getting started, optimum group size, basic mutual covenants, leadership, and so forth, which help a group begin and faithfully sustain its practice of lectio. The goal of these details is to create and sustain a flexible lectio structure for a satisfying, growth-inducing, and Christ-centered small-group process, while also supporting each member in the difficult work of being a Christian in the midst of life. The tools presented here build on and provide a framework for the four elements of community life supporting individuals, discussed in chapter 2.

Many groups depend for their structure and discipline on the presence of a leader figure, someone who explicitly sets and maintains the ground rules. However, in an independent and cooperatively led group, such as the one recommended here for effective lectio, it is necessary for all the group members to share responsibility for the establishment and continuance of group life, although in assuming mutual leadership, we may feel a bit out of our depth, a bit like Jeremiah:

> Ah, Lord, truly I do not know how to speak, for I am only [a participant]. (Jer. 1:6–7)

However, a few basic practices presented here can make this shared group leadership much easier, enabling all lectio group members to participate in knowledge and responsibility for group life.

Getting Started

For many of us, the process of getting a group together seems overwhelming, if not impossible. We're not sure how to go about it, we're shy to ask others, and sure no one will be interested. We feel it may be an imposition; we know it's been tried before. . . . The list of anxieties goes on forever.

The best way to begin any group is to pray about it. If you have been reading this book and are interested in trying to begin a lectio group, consider that God has planted that interest in your heart, and God is probably matching it with some unspoken desire in the hearts of others you know. The first step of any good action is always praying to God to bring it to perfection. Pray specifically that God will bring others to join you, and pray to be open and responsive to what God is calling you to do as the group begins to come into being. Everything that follows then takes place in the light and under the strength of that prayer, so keep your eyes open!

It is a good idea to find a partner, or buddy, to help you in the initial stages. If the vision is yours alone at present, find at least one other who shares your dream and desire for a lectio group, and work together on it. If you and your spouse share this vision, you may wish to seek another couple to join you in the initial gathering of the group. Then decide how many people you need as a minimum. This number is probably smaller than you think: five or six is a good starting number; twelve is probably too many for one group.

Think and pray about people you know who might be interested in this sort of thing, and propose it to them. Don't presume that people won't be interested; go ahead and ask them! Talk about your plans with enthusiasm, and invite others to join you. And as people agree to join you, ask them to share their enthusiasm with others. Personal contact—sharing the contagion of your excitement—works better as a recruiting device than any number of bulletin announcements or form letters. Some people will not be interested, for a variety of reasons, but don't let that get you down. A few will be delighted, and that's all you need.

When you talk with others, don't understate your hopes or your commitment. Let them know how important you expect the lectio group to be for your spiritual journey, and be honest about the level of commitment you will want from members. You may be surprised how many people would rather join a group that really intends a serious (though not solemn) commitment than one that expects only a half-hearted response. Also, don't underestimate the value of diverse gifts and temperaments in a lectio group. A group may be much richer for having a variety of viewpoints. You'll find that the basic criteria you'll want to present to potential members are simply "Are you really seeking God?" and "Does this particular method seem sufficiently fruitful to you that you would be willing to commit to it for a time?"

When you've gathered enough people who are interested, decide on a time and place for the first meeting and make sure that everyone can come. That first meeting should be an exploratory one, in which those present actually practice a lectio experience and then discuss possible covenant items (discussed in the following section). By the end of that meeting, you will want to reach agreement on basic format, timing, and covenant items.

The basic format for regular meetings is flexible, depending on members' needs and desires. A group may wish to combine the lectio experience with other elements, such as additional (contemplative or intercessory) prayer time, spiritual reading and study, life-sharing and support, joining together in a meal, working together on a service project or common task, or some combination. Also, it is not impossible to undertake a group lectio session before the normal meeting of a regular church committee (say, the parish council, vestry, or board of elders), or to include it as part of a support group agenda. Just be sure to keep the lectio process intact, not mixing it with other elements during the period of lectio itself.

Timing involves several elements, including the length of the initial commitment as well as the frequency and duration of meetings. The optimum frequency probably is weekly, although the group may decide on something else that is more suitable for them. The lectio process itself takes twenty-five to forty minutes, depending on the size of the group. Of course, if additional elements are added, the meetings will be correspondingly longer. Generally, it is good to make an initial commitment to the process for a specific period of months, to give it a chance to take hold before attempting to evaluate it.

Before leaving the exploratory meeting, you will want to give everyone present the opportunity to commit to the ongoing group or not. And you will want to schedule the next (regular) meeting with those who have agreed to join. You're on your way!

Covenanting Together

A mutually led group needs to begin with free and frank discussion of people's hopes and what their commitment to each other will be. If several members have different sets of expectations, the result is bound to be less than satisfactory. When we choose to come together in a small group, the promise, or *covenant*, we make to each other helps shape and direct our life together. It is as if we were building a home together—a task that is near-impossible if each person has a different set of plans.

> Come to him, a living stone . . . , and like living stones let yourselves be built into a spiritual house. (1 Pet. 2:4a, 5a)

Our covenant helps move us from vague intention to directed and mutual commitment. Since everyone in the group is to be a full participant, each taking responsibility for good content and mutual sharing, it is very important that all participate fully in negotiating the covenant agreement during the first meeting. The covenant agreement includes basic lectio principles and practices as well as practical groundrules established by the group, involving both content and practice of meetings.

THE CONTENT OF MEETINGS

The exploratory meeting should begin with a practice of group lectio. Then it is useful to discuss meeting content issues raised in chapter 2, assuring that they are understood and can be accepted by each member, or will be modified in some way. Particular issues that should be aired and agreed upon include these:

> Accept ourselves and our lives as we are, but consent
> not to be confined by the present.

Allow our hearts to be formed by lectio's structure by:
staying with the words of the Scripture passage;
staying with the outline of the process (in chart 1);
taking time to prepare and close every session; and
staying open to the unknown

Practice a balance of silence and word. Also assure that everyone listens and everyone speaks.

Speak the truth in love by
speaking for oneself rather than "at" others; and
welcoming and airing diverse points of view.

Admit strong emotions to ourselves and appropriately with others.

Practice confidentiality.

THE PRACTICE OF MEETINGS

In addition to the content of lectio sessions, the covenant will include other practical items. It will be helpful to discuss and agree on an approach to each of the following matters:

1. How often, how long, and where will the group meet?

a. Will it begin and end promptly on time, or how much leeway can be allowed for members to feel comfortable?

b. If members' homes are used for meetings, will there be rotation among homes, or is it easier to meet routinely in the same place? Would everyone be more comfortable in a "neutral" place, for example, the church library? If refreshments are to be served (they need not be), how will that responsibility be shared?

2. How will leadership be shared? It is strongly urged that the group rotate leadership among all the members so that everyone feels a sense of ownership for what happens in the group, but there are different ways to handle this. Will the leader change every session, or every four or six sessions (for example)? Will the designated leader be responsible both for selecting the Scripture and guiding the lectio *and* for assigning

these tasks for the next rotation? Or will these tasks rotate among the members separately?

3. When will new members be permitted to join? If the group decides to accept new members at *any* time, there may be difficulty establishing a sense of shared group identity and trust. On the other hand, if the group *never* accepts new members, it is likely to grow stale and ingrown. What procedure would the members like to follow regarding accepting new members?

4. What will be the group's life span? How long is the initial commitment members make to each other and the group? It is well to plan that after about four meetings you will set aside time for special discussion of how the group is going, and whether any modifications need to be made in covenant items or group practices. However, a basic period for the initial commitment should be established at the first meeting. This period should not exceed one year nor be less than three months. After that time, the group should plan to have a full meeting evaluating how the process has gone for them, celebrating successes and acknowledging necessary losses. Group members may wish to terminate the group, or perhaps some will leave and others stay and find new members to join. If the group will continue, there needs to be decision as to what form it will take and how long the next period of commitment will be.

5. Is each member willing to commit to pray for the others between meetings? If regular prayer for each other is included in the covenant, the members may find their common life greatly enriched.

Ideally, the group will discuss all these issues, at least briefly, during the first meeting, and come to a consensus about methods of operation at the end of that meeting. It may help to write up a summary of what was agreed, and give everyone a copy. Remember, the objective of developing a covenant is no more and no less than to help shape the life of the group. As such, it is an early means of practicing the theology of lectio that says that life and prayer are mutually influential: We get to experience "prayer in action" in the process of making decisions and working together.

Note that the intent is not that the group spend the first several meetings arguing about elements of a covenant, thereby effectively using discussion to avoid prayer and reflection on Scripture together. To the contrary, an early airing of these foundational dynamics will help create prayerful structure that will enable optimum openness to God and each other.

Sharing Leadership

How does one actually take leadership responsibility during a group lectio session? The leadership of a Christian small group is quite different from our usual ideas about leadership. First, we remember that Jesus taught us about a form of leadership that involves *serving* others:

> But Jesus called them to him and said, "You know that the rulers of the Gentiles lord it over them, and their great ones are tyrants over them. It will not be so among you; but whoever wishes to be great among you must be your servant." (Matt. 20:25–26)

Thus for us the marks of a good leader are not so much expertise and power as willingness to be oneself and be open to God's Spirit. The small-group leader stands alongside, not above, helping each member discover for him- or herself where God is leading. Also, in a small group, the members grow in Christ primarily through interaction and discovery, rather than through instruction and advice. As we saw in chapter 2 on community life, each member of the group has an essential contribution. The leader's goal is primarily to facilitate the full contribution of all members during the session.

In short, the main purpose of the leader is to be available and helpful to others through the Spirit. Thus, the primary tasks of leadership in a lectio group are four:

- Pray
- Prepare
- Guide
- Care

PRAY

Prayer undergirds and strengthens the leader and the group. It provides wisdom and sensitivity to the whisperings of the Spirit as the group listens and speaks. Prayer is useful not only in establishing and maintaining openness within the group, but also in aiding one's own openness to God and the group and at other times. Prayer aids each member and the group as a whole between and before meetings, and can assist in anything else with which you feel you need help. Each meeting's designated leader will find his or her work much lightened when it is set in the context of personal prayer.

PREPARE

Preparation for group lectio is relatively simple, but it does include the following responsibilities:

1. Anticipating and scheduling time for the various components of the meeting. For example, if there is time set aside for open sharing at the beginning and end, approximately how much time will be allowed for that? What is the minimum time needed for the full lectio process? How long is the babysitter available? If refreshments are available, when should the group adjourn to a less formal mode?

2. Praying over and reviewing the Lectio process until it becomes completely familiar. The leader might do this by practicing a solitary lectio on the proposed passage ahead of time.

3. Seeking others' help as appropriate. For example, it might be thoughtful to let others know ahead of time if you plan to ask them to read the passage.

Before the meeting, the leader should make sure that the chairs are in a true circle so that everyone is fully included physically. And don't forget to bring either your Bible, with the passage that you have selected marked, or a typed copy of the passage that can be handed to the other readers.

Take time at the beginning to relax yourself and the others—physically as well as mentally and emotionally—since everyone needs some time to make the transition from their busy lives into this privileged time of meeting God. Finally, remember that God is in your midst as the group gathers together.

GUIDE

Guidance is the task of facilitating the flow of the lectio time. The following are some points you, as leader, will want to keep in mind:

1. It may be helpful to obtain a watch that tells exactly when two or three minutes have passed so that you needn't be anxious about how long to leave for silences.

2. During sharing, it may be necessary gently to interrupt participants, to ask them to stay with the given lectio structure. Be prepared to do this without aggression or anger, but with firmness and confidence in the process.

3. Always honor each person's right to pass at any time; never force anyone to share.

4. At each stage, you will want briefly to repeat the instructions for that stage, as set out in chapter 1.

5. As leader, you may wish to take a particularly supportive role in response to the group members' contributions. This is not in any sense to suggest that you will respond formally or at length, but rather that you may simply want to make affirming sounds or thank each member for sharing.

Do the best you can, and be flexible. Remember, God is the main guide for your group at every moment.

CARE

Caring is basically the task of attending thoughtfully and fully to each and every member of the group, demonstrated by sensitive listening and brief responses. It may help you, just before the meeting, to hold each member imaginatively in your heart and up to God, specifically praying that this person might find his or her personal good in this meeting.

Caring also means responding to the needs of a particular situation or moment. For instance, in the early meetings, if the group members do not know each other, the leader needs to take the time simply to make sure everyone knows each other's name. Similarly, if someone begins coughing violently, or there is a loud noise outside, there is nothing wrong with interrupting the regular process to acknowledge what is going on. Your best gift of caring is to bring yourself as you are to the group, and be as natural as only you can.

Obviously, all of the preceding "leadership" tasks should be practiced by all members of the group, but they are the special responsibility and opportunity of the one who is leading the lectio.

Summary

The foundational principle of lectio groups is openness to the ongoing conversion of the Spirit of God and attentive expectancy to the creative headship of Christ to whom we belong. This is easier said than done, and attention to a few basic matters can be a big help.

If you feel the desire to begin a lectio group, trust that God has given you that desire and be enthusiastic in your contacts.

It is well to begin a group with a full and frank discussion of how you will conduct yourselves. Gain agreement on a basic format and procedures, and commit to each other that each will assume responsibility for the life of the group.

Be aware that mutual leadership is not so much a matter of expertise as it is of loving concern, of prayer, and of supporting one another in everything. May this practice empower you!

CHAPTER 4

Good Beginning Lectio Texts

Lectio texts can be chosen from any reflective source, even those not in Scripture. However, the emphasis is on Scripture as a privileged place of meeting God. Even so, it is clearly the case that within the Bible itself there are many different types of literature, some of which are more suitable for devotional purposes than others. As a group or individual becomes more and more familiar with the heart and rhythm of lectio, it will become the case that *any* text, or indeed any event, can become a place for meeting the living God. In the meantime, it only makes sense to start with those passages that are most helpful and easily accessible for our purpose.

Given the particular focus of our group lectio mode, the most fruitful texts are ones from the Gospels or the Psalms that have strong action verbs or concrete images. Images such as planting seed, touching a hem, or searching for a lost coin are vivid ways of thinking about God's presence. For example, an excellent text is Luke 5:4–7, about the fishermen/disciples lowering their nets again for a large catch of fish. Or perhaps you might explore a passage such as Psalm 23:2, suggesting God inviting us to rest in green pastures and beside still waters.

Strong action verbs such as *cry out, come, call forth,* or *leap* help us appropriate the dynamic quality of God in our midst. Examples might include Psalm 22:1–2, which expresses a sense of being abandoned by God with such words as *crying, forsaking, groaning.*

Or we might choose the vivid image in Mark 10:47–48, in which the blind beggar hears and shouts, is ordered to silence, and yet cries even more loudly.

By and large, it is well to avoid strongly theological or cognitive texts, such as some of the New Testament epistles, as well as historical or ritual texts, such as Judges or Leviticus. It is rarely helpful to choose a passage loaded with words like *sin, salvation, repent,* because we think we ought to know what such words mean, and that tends to block the spontaneous response to God here at our side. For example, group lectio would probably not be fruitful on a text such as this one from Romans (3:23–24):

> All have sinned and fall short of the glory of God; they are now justified by his grace as a gift, through the redemption that is in Christ Jesus."

This *is* a central passage for Bible *study*, and in the right teaching context can be very meaningful indeed, but it is far from optimum for the usual lectio group.

As they start, groups will find the most helpful material in the Gospels, especially Matthew, Mark, and Luke, and in the Psalms, especially those with strong emotional energy. The purpose of lectio is to realize and bring home the essence of basic theological truths, but the method of lectio is to do so through the means of direct engagement from the heart with the Holy Spirit of God. These suggested texts help evoke responses and inner dialogue at the level of the heart.

The second major ingredient in selecting an appropriate text for group lectio is length. The text should not exceed ten verses, and may be as short as one verse. There should be enough words to give group members some flexibility in selection, but not so many words that the complete text cannot be held in the mind. The goal is to give members an opportunity to choose only one word or a short phrase, not to teach a whole lesson. Sometimes, you might even choose a portion of a story, rather than the whole thing, because it is not so important that we "get the point," as that we make a contact with God that relates to our lives.

For example, one of the most moving texts in the Gospels is that of the paralyzed man brought to Jesus by his friends, Mark 2:1–12, but all twelve verses are really too long for an effective lectio time. So the leader might instead select only a verse or two that might evoke a strong sense of connection with God, for example verses 1a–2:

> It was reported that he was at home. So many gathered around that there was no longer room for them, not even in front of the door; and he was speaking the word to them.

Or perhaps one might choose verses 11–12:

> [Jesus said] "I say to you, stand up, take your mat and go to your home." And he stood up, and immediately took the mat and went out before all of them, so that they were all amazed and glorified God, saying, "We have never seen anything like this!"

The goal of lectio is to help us incarnate a way of conversing with God about the specific life issues we have, in such a way that transformation can occur through God's work in our midst. Throughout the centuries, Christians have found the words of the Bible to be so rich in the vital presence of God that lectio *divina* (meaning holy Scripture) has been the central reflective basis for lectio. However, when lectio functions as intended in our hearts, it begins to predispose us for dialogue with God in reflective engagement with many other sources. Always, the writings and sayings of "holy" persons have been known to be important supplements to the Bible. And it is hoped that in time the mode of reflective dialogue with God will be initiated even by the events of our lives themselves, as discussed in chapter 5.

The remainder of this chapter consists of sample texts that might be used for a beginning group. When the members gradually gain a feel for the type of texts that work best for them, they will certainly want to branch out beyond these. Sample texts are offered from the Gospel and other New Testament, Hebrew Scriptures, and spiritual classics.

SAMPLE GOSPEL TEXTS

Matthew 5:13–16a

You are the salt of the earth. But if salt has lost its taste, how can its saltiness be restored? It is no longer good for anything, but is thrown out and trampled underfoot. You are the light of the world. A city built on a hill cannot be hid. No one after lighting a lamp puts it under the bushel basket, but on the lampstand, and it gives light to all in the house. In the same way, let your light shine.

Matthew 11:28–30

Come to me, all you that are weary and are carrying heavy burdens, and I will give you rest. Take my yoke upon you and learn from me; for I am gentle and humble in heart, and you will find rest for your souls. For my yoke is easy and my burden is light.

Matthew 13:3b–8

Listen! A sower went out to sow. And as he sowed, some seeds fell on the path, and the birds came and ate them up. Other seeds fell on rocky ground, where they did not have much soil, and they sprang up quickly, since they had no depth of the soil. But when the sun rose, they were scorched; and since they had no root, they withered away. Other seeds fell among thorns, and the thorns grew up and choked them. Other seeds fell on good soil and brought forth grain—some a hundredfold, some sixty, some thirty.

Matthew 13:31–33

He put before them another parable: "The kingdom of heaven is like a mustard seed that someone took and sowed in the field; it is the smallest of all the seeds, but when it has grown it is the greatest of shrubs and becomes a tree, so that the birds of the air come and make nests in its branches."

He told them another parable: "The kingdom of heaven is like yeast that a woman took and mixed in with three measures of flour until all of it was leavened."

Mark 1:35–37

In the morning, while it was still very dark, [Jesus] got up and went out to a deserted place, and there he prayed. And Simon and his companions hunted for him. When they found him, they said to him: "Everyone is searching for you!"

Mark 4:26–28

He also said, "The kingdom of God is as if someone would scatter seed on the ground, and would sleep and rise night and day, and the seed would sprout and grow, he does not know how. The earth produces of itself, first the stalk, then the head, then the full grain in the head."

Mark 11:2–9

[Jesus said to two of his disciples:] Go into the village ahead of you, and immediately as you enter it, you will find tied there a colt that has never been ridden; untie it and bring it. If anyone says to you, "Why are you doing this?" just say this, "The Lord needs it and will send it back here immediately." They went away and found a colt tied near a door. . . . Then they brought the colt to Jesus and threw their cloaks on it; and he sat on it. Many people spread their cloaks on the road, and others spread leafy branches that they had cut in the fields. Then those who went ahead and those who followed were shouting, "Hosanna! Blessed is the one who comes in the name of the Lord!"

Luke 3:10–15a

And the crowds asked him, "What then should we do?" In reply [John] said to them, "Whoever has two coats must share with anyone who has none; and whoever has food must do likewise." Even tax collectors came to be baptized, and they asked him, "Teacher, what should we do?" He said to them, "Collect no more than the amount prescribed for you." Soldiers also asked him, "And we, what should we do?" He said to them, "Do not extort money from anyone by threats or false accusation, and be satisfied with your wages." And the people were filled with expectation.

Luke 5:4–7

When he had finished speaking, he said to Simon, "Put out into the deep water, and let down your nets for a catch." Simon answered, "Master, we have worked hard all night long but have caught nothing. Yet if you say so, I will let down the nets." When they had done this, they caught so many fish that their nets were beginning to break. So they signaled their partners in the other boat to come and help them. And they came and filled both boats, so that they began to sink.

Luke 7:44b–47

[Jesus said] Do you see this woman? I entered your house; you gave me no water for my feet, but she has bathed my feet with her tears and dried them with her hair. You gave me no kiss, but from the time I came in she has not stopped kissing my feet. You did not anoint my head with oil, but she has anointed my feet with ointment. Therefore, I tell you, her sins, which were many, have been forgiven—for she has shown great love.

Luke 9:1–6

Then Jesus called the twelve together and gave them power and authority over all demons and to cure diseases, and he sent them out to proclaim the kingdom of God and to heal. He said to them, "Take nothing for your journey, no staff, nor bag, nor bread, nor money—not even an extra tunic. Whatever house you enter, stay there, and leave from there. Wherever they do not welcome you, as you are leaving that town, shake the dust off your feet, as a testimony against them." They departed and went through the villages, bringing the good news and curing diseases everywhere.

Luke 14:16–21

Someone gave a great dinner and invited many. At the time for the dinner he sent his slave to say to those who had been invited, "Come, for everything is ready now." But they all alike began to make excuses. The first said to him, "I have just bought a piece of land, and I must go out and see it; please accept my regrets." Another said, "I have bought five yoke of oxen, and I am going to try them out; please accept my regrets." Another said, "I have just been married, and therefore I cannot come." So the slave returned and reported this to his master.

John 1:35–39a

The next day John again was standing with two of his disciples, and as he watched Jesus walk by, he exclaimed, "Look, here is the Lamb of God!" The two disciples heard him say this, and they followed Jesus.

When Jesus turned and saw them following, he said to them, "What are you looking for?" They said to him, "Rabbi," (which translated means Teacher) "where are you staying?" He said to them, "Come and see."

John 15:15–16a

[Jesus said] I do not call you servants any longer, because the servant does not know what the master is doing; but I have called you friends, because I have made known to you everything that I have heard from my Father. You did not choose me, but I chose you. And I appointed you to go and bear fruit, fruit that will last.

OTHER NEW TESTAMENT POSSIBILITIES

Acts 3:4–8

Peter looked intently at (the crippled man), as did John, and said, "Look at us!" And he fixed his attention on them, expecting to receive something from them. But Peter said, "I have no silver or gold, but what I have I give you; in the name of Jesus Christ of Nazareth, stand up and walk." And he took him by the right hand and raised him up; and immediately his feet and ankles were made strong. Jumping up, he stood and began to walk, and he entered into the temple with them, walking and leaping, and praising God.

Acts 17:24–27a

[Paul said] The God who made the world and everything in it, [the one] who is Lord of heaven and earth, does not live in shrines made by human hands, nor is [God] served by human hands, as though he needed anything, since [God] gives to all mortals life and breath and all things. . . . [God does this] so that [we] would search for God and perhaps grope for him and find him—though indeed [God] is not far from each one of us. "For in [God] we live and move and have our being."

Colossians 3:14–16a

Above all clothe yourself with love, which binds everything together in perfect harmony. And let the peace of Christ rule in your hearts, to which indeed you were called in the one body. And be thankful. Let the word of Christ dwell in you richly.

SAMPLE TEXTS FROM THE HEBREW SCRIPTURES

Genesis 1:21–22a

So God created the great sea monsters and every living creature that moves, of every kind, with which the waters swarm, and every winged bird of every kind. And God saw that it was good. God blessed them, saying, "Be fruitful."

Genesis 28:11–12, 16

[Jacob] came to a certain place and stayed there for the night, because the sun had set. Taking one of the stones of the place, he put it under his head and lay down in that place. And he dreamed that there was a ladder set up on the earth, the top of it reaching to heaven; and the angels of God were ascending and descending on it. . . . Then Jacob woke from his sleep and said, "Surely the Lord is in this place—and I did not know it!"

Exodus 15:1–2

Then Moses and the Israelites sang this song to the Lord: "I will sing to the Lord, for [God] has triumphed gloriously; horse and rider he has thrown into the sea. The Lord is my strength and my might, and [God] has become my salvation; this is my God and I will praise him, my [ancestor's] God and I will exalt him."

Deuteronomy 30:11–14

Surely, this commandment that I am commanding you today is not too hard for you, nor is it too far away. It is not in heaven, that you should say, "Who will go up to heaven for us, and get it for us so that we may hear it and observe it?" . . . No, the word is very near to you; it is in your mouth and in your heart for you to observe.

I Samuel 3:9

Therefore Eli said to Samuel, "Go, lie down; and if [God] calls you, you shall say, 'Speak, Lord, for your servant is listening.'"

I Kings 19:11–13

[The angel] said, "Go out and stand on the mountain before the Lord, for the Lord is about to pass by." Now there was a great wind, so strong that it was splitting mountains . . . but the Lord was not in the wind; and after the wind an earthquake, but the Lord was not in the earthquake; and after the earthquake a fire, but the Lord was not in the fire; and after the fire a sound of sheer silence. When Elijah heard it, he wrapped his face in his mantle and went out and stood at the entrance of the cave. Then there came a voice to him that said, "What are you doing here?"

Esther 4:15–17

Then Esther said in reply to Mordecai, "Go, gather all (our people) to be found in Susa, and hold a fast on my behalf, and neither eat nor drink for three days, night or day. I and my maids will also fast as you do. After that I will go to the king, though it is against the law; and if I perish, I perish." Mordecai then went away and did everything as Esther had ordered him.

Psalm 46:10–11

Be still, and know that I am God! I am exalted among the nations, I am exalted in the earth. The Lord of hosts is with us; the God of Jacob is our refuge.

Psalm 95:6–8a

O come, let us worship and bow down, let us kneel before the Lord our Maker! For [this] is our God and we are the people of [the] pasture and the sheep of [God's] hand. O that today you would listen to [God's] voice! Do not harden your hearts.

Psalm 127:1–2

Unless the Lord builds the house, those who build it labor in vain. Unless the Lord guards the city, the guard keeps watch in vain. It is in vain that you rise up early and go late to rest, eating the bread of anxious toil; for [God] gives sleep to (the) beloved.

Ecclesiastes 11:1–2, 5; 12:1

Send out your bread upon the waters, for after many days you will get it back. Divide your means seven ways, or even eight, for you do not know what . . . [may] happen on earth. . . . Just as you do not know how the breath comes to the bones in the mother's womb, so you do not know the work of God, who makes everything. . . . Remember your creator.

Song of Solomon 2:10–13

My beloved speaks and says to me: "Arise my love, my fair one, and come away; for now the winter is past, the rain is over and gone. The flowers appear on the earth; the time of singing has come, and the voice of the turtledove is heard in our land. The figtree puts forth its figs, and the vines are in blossom; they give forth fragrance. Arise, my love, my fair one, and come away [with me].

Isaiah 55:10–12a

For as the rain and the snow come down from heaven, and do not return there until they have watered the earth, making it bring forth and sprout, giving seed to the sower and bread to the eater, so shall my word be that goes out from my mouth; it shall not return to me empty, but shall accomplish that which I purpose and succeed in the thing for which I sent it. For you shall go out in joy and be led back in peace.

Ezekiel 36:26–27a

A new heart I will give you, and a new spirit I will put within you; and I will remove from your body the heart of stone and give you a heart of flesh. I will put my spirit within you.

Hosea 2:14–15a

Therefore I will now allure her, and bring her into the wilderness, and speak tenderly to her. From there I will give her her vineyards, and make the Valley of Achor a door of hope. There she shall respond as in the days of her youth.

Joel 2:28–29

Then afterward I will pour out my spirit on all flesh; your sons and your daughters shall prophesy, your old men shall dream dreams, and your young men shall see visions. Even on the male and female slaves, in those days, I will pour out my spirit.

Zephaniah 3:17

The Lord, your God, is in your midst, a warrior who gives victory; [God] will rejoice over you with gladness, [God] will renew you in love and exult over you with loud singing.

Zechariah 2:4–5, 10

[The angel] said, "Run, say to that young [one]: Jerusalem shall be inhabited like villages without walls, because of the multitude of people and animals in it. For I will be a wall of fire all around it," says the Lord, "and I will be the glory within it. . . . Sing and rejoice, O daughter of Zion! For lo, I will come and dwell in your midst.

Malachi 3:7b, 10

"Return to me, and I will return to you," says the Lord of hosts. But you say, "How shall we return?". . . "Bring the full tithe into the storehouse, that there may be food in my house, and thus put me to the test," says the Lord of hosts; "see if I will not open the windows of heaven for you and pour down for you an overflowing blessing."

Sirach 1:1–4

All wisdom is from the Lord, and with [God] it remains forever. The sands of the sea, the drops of rain, and the days of eternity—who can count them? The height of heaven, the breadth of the earth, the abyss and wisdom—who can search them out? Wisdom was created before everything, and prudent understanding from eternity.

SAMPLE TEXTS FROM SPIRITUAL CLASSICS

St. Augustine of Hippo (354–430 A.D., Egypt), *Confessions*

I shall know you, my knower, I shall know you even as I am known. Power of my soul, enter into it and fit it for yourself, so that you may have it and hold it without spot or wrinkle. This is my hope. (Book 10, chapter 1, page 229; Image, 1960)

St. Benedict of Nursia (360–433 A.D., Italy), *Rule*

Be chaste, temperate, and merciful. Let mercy triumph over judgment so that [you] too may win mercy. . . . Use prudence and avoid extremes; otherwise by rubbing too hard to remove the rust, [you] may break the vessel. (64:9–12; Liturgical Press, 1980)

St. Bernard of Clairvaux (1090–1153 A.D., France), *On Loving God*

[Our] frequent needs oblige [us] to invoke God more often and approach God more frequently. This intimacy moves [us] to taste and discover how sweet the Lord is. Tasting God's sweetness entices [us] more to pure love than does the urgency of our own needs. (IX:26; Cistercian Publications CF13, 1974)

Hildegard of Bingen (1098–1179 A.D., Germany), *Scivias* (Know the ways)

For the soul passes through the body just as sap passes through a tree. What does this mean? It is through the sap that a tree is green, produces flowers, and then fruit. And how does the fruit come to maturity? The sun warms it, the rain waters it, and it is perfected by the mildness of the air. The mercy of the grace of God will make a person bright as the sun, the breadth of the Holy Spirit will water the person just as the rain, and thus discretion will lead the person to the perfection of good fruits just like the mildness of the air does for the tree. (Vision Four:25, page 55; Bear & Co., 1986)

Anonymous (fourteenth century, England) *The Cloud of Unknowing*

And so diligently persevere [in this prayer] until you feel joy in it. For in the beginning it is usual to feel nothing but a kind of darkness about your mind, or as it were, a cloud of unknowing. You will seem to know nothing and to feel nothing except a naked intent toward God in the depths of your being. . . . Learn to be at home in this darkness. Return to it as often as you can, letting your spirit cry out to God whom you love. (Chapter 3, pages 48–49; Image, 1973)

Julian(a) of Norwich, (1342–1420 A.D., England),
Showings **(long text)**

And then I saw that only pain blames and punishes, and our courteous Lord comforts and succours, and always he is kindly disposed to the soul, loving and longing to bring us to his bliss. (Chapter 51, page 271; Paulist, 1978)

Brother Lawrence of the Resurrection (1611–1691 A.D., France),
The Practice of the Presence of God

Comfort yourself with thoughts of [God] as often as you can. Lift up your heart to [God] sometimes when you are at meals or in society; the least little remembrance will always be pleasing to [God]. There is no need to cry very loudly, for [God] is nearer to us than we think. (Fourth Letter, page 68; Templegate, 1974)

Jean-Pierre De Caussade (1675–1751 A.D., France),
The Sacrament of the Present Moment

The present moment holds infinite riches beyond your wildest dreams but you will only enjoy them to the extent of your faith and love. The more a soul loves, the more it longs, the more it hopes, the more it finds. The will of God is manifest in each moment, an immense ocean which the heart only fathoms in so far as it overflows with faith, trust, and love. (Chapter 9, page 62; Harper, 1989)

Thomas Kelly (twentieth century, United States),
A Testament of Devotion

The outer distractions of our interests reflect an inner lack of integration of our own lives. We are trying to be several selves at once, without all our selves being organized by a single, mastering Life within us. ("The Simplification of Life," page 114; Harper, 1941)

Evelyn Underhill (twentieth century, England), *Abba*

Thy Kingdom come! We open our gates to the Perfect, and entreat its transfiguring presence; redeeming our . . . disharmonies. We face the awful contrast between the Actual and the Real, and acknowledge our need of deliverance. . . . The Kingdom is the serenity of God already enfolding us, and seeking to penetrate and redeem the whole of this created order. (Chapter IV, page 28; Forward Movement, 1940)

CHAPTER 5

Lectio Texts from Life

Chapter 4 offered examples of lectio texts, primarily from scripture but also from spiritual classics. There it was suggested that appropriate texts for lectio can be found in reflective engagement with many sources. The practice of lectio using scripture is intended to form us in spiritual growth, with the aim of deepened receptivity to God's very life in our innermost being. Indeed, it is hoped that lectio divina gradually enables us to find even the ordinary events of our lives to be "texts" for engagement with God. This chapter explores *lectio on life*, the use of life experiences as lectio texts. After the basic concept is presented, a specific method is proposed and a group example given.

Lectio as a New Way of Seeing

As a personal rhythm of lectio experience begins to emerge, group members will begin to sense some subtle new awareness. Members come to the group meeting with a certain expectancy—or maybe even a kind of superstitious awe—based on the aggregate of past experiences. How astonishing it is to discover, time after time, that God actually meets us in this process. How amazing it is that, even when we don't know exactly what our needs are, as we settle down into the quiet reflection of group lectio, we receive something of strength or hope for our life. How gracious that this apparently new, yet completely ordinary, element is so consistently added to our situations when we offer them to God!

GOD FOUND IN LIFE AS IN SCRIPTURE

We return again and again to the recognition that lectio is about the intersection of human and divine, or prayer and life. In lectio, we experience these "opposites" as somehow unified, and we receive guidance for the best next step we can take to express this unity in our situation. Lectio does not force us to choose between intimacy with God and an active life in the world, but instead enables us to integrate those two important poles of human experience.

Lectio does not allow us to refuse or ignore difficulties in our particular settings; rather it invites us to offer them to God for transformation. We begin to gain a sense that God is teaching us exactly what we need to be and do at this moment, within the context of our given circumstances and experiences. So often we may have felt that we could be good and holy if only we did not have to deal with adolescent children or elderly parents. If only we did not have to cope with that drunken boss, we could really get our act together. If only we were not so crippled by childhood abuse that we suffer continuously from the compulsion to eat, then we could really be something special. If only, if only! And yet in lectio, and especially in lectio on life, we discover with amazement that God is calling us to love and serve and be embraced, just where we are!

Lectio teaches us that it is misguided to believe that God can't understand the complexities or earthiness of our life issues; rather every actual life situation has a prayerful invitation, when we are attentive. It is delightful to imagine Jesus himself learning these lessons of lectio on life, finding himself meeting the Father in the most unexpected places! Something like this is suggested in Jesus's encounters with two non-Jews, in whom Jesus is amazed to find God already at work. The Canaanite woman whose daughter is ill is not put off by Jesus's rebuke that food meant for the children should not be given to dogs; instead she bravely responds that even the dogs receive table scraps! And Jesus is delighted, knowing he has encountered God unexpectedly in this saucy but believing woman, and sends her home assured that her daughter will be well. (Matt. 15:21–28) The incident with the Roman centurion whose slave is sick is similar; Jesus is moved when he encounters such simple faith:

> But when Jesus was not far from the house, the centurion sent friends to say to him, "Lord, do not trouble yourself, for I am not worthy to have you come under my roof; therefore I did not presume to come to you. But

only speak the word, and let my servant be healed, [for I know your authority]." (Luke 7:1–10)

Again, Jesus is amazed. He is in wonder at the unexpected encounter with God's life moving in this foreigner, and again he lets his power go forth in cooperation with that already present. Such images are a bit fanciful because, of course, Jesus himself is God, but they highlight nuances of earthly life taught us in our Lord's incarnation.

Lectio invites us to change our way of seeing things, to allow ourselves to be surprised by encounters with God in unlikely places. We are no longer stuck alone in the middle of disaster, nor are we lifted far above the fray. We are still in the middle of our troubles, but now there are options, possibilities beyond our imagining, because we are not alone. We begin to look for God in Christ in every event, encounter, moment. We begin to sense the tangible, yet hidden, presence of the Kingdom, which although not yet fulfilled, is somehow already here.

What started as a willingness to believe that the living God might be found in scripture is extended to a willingness to believe that the living God might also be found in creation. God is Creator; should not the very structure of the world somehow reveal the mark—indeed the presence—of the Artist? Maybe it is true, as C. S. Lewis observes, that "the world is filled up with God. Our task is simply to come awake and stay awake."[1] If so, lectio is a marvelous way to "read" life as well as scripture, with the same result of transforming encounters with God.

Lectio can be done using life events as texts, as well as scripture. Just as the pages of scripture are given for us to read, mark, learn, and inwardly digest, so can the incidents of each day be given for reflection. Just as Christ is encountered in scripture with a word of strength and hope, so may Christ be encountered in life situations with a transforming word. It is surely not a surprise that the deep intention of lectio is a transfer of its lessons from book to life. And we may wish to explore this possibility directly, by the practice of lectio on life situations themselves, as well as to reap the natural fruits that come about in ongoing lectio divina.

Of course, life is not a substitute for scripture (nor vice versa), and it is well to sustain devotional reflection on scripture whether or not devotional reflection on life is deliberately added. Both exercises express and incarnate a new way of seeing and hearing that involves a capacity to respond to God in one's midst, wherever one finds oneself.

Lectio on life is based on the conviction that God is present in every single event, encounter, and thought. We find urgent invitation to lectio on life in the pivotal experience of the Hebrews wandering the desert, forced by thirst to cry out their pain: "Is God among us or not?" And significantly, this cry is met by the generous response of living water flowing forth from the "rocks" of daily life experience. (Exod. 17:7) Is God among us or not? In every tiny moment and obscure place, God is waiting to surprise and delight us, when we learn to see and hear. And when we do see and hear, our lives are transformed: We have new choices and we become co-creators in the coming of God's Kingdom.

HOLDING LIFE AND PRAYER IN TENSION

All Christian spiritual practices combine prayer and life to some extent, but this connection is a particularly marked characteristic of lectio and its sources. Each Christian spiritual practice attracts those who find it an especially fruitful way to God, and the reason for so much diversity in spiritual practices is that there is so much diversity in temperament, timing, and need. It is well, therefore to emphasize that lectio's method of prayer is definitely oriented to the *kataphatic*, or physical, end of the spectrum: It is a way that values images and engagement with the many. Yet it also involves the *apophatic*, or imageless side—in rhythmic *interchange* with images. It rests in the unknowable and unnameable God. Lectio, however, does not aim to stay in the wordless and imageless dimension, as do so many modern spiritual exercises. Rather it always draws us back into life experience as an essential part of the prayer, because its goal is always the growing integration of prayer into life, of life into prayer.

Because lectio is so earthy, it may be thought that it is not mystical. Yet some participants will initially find it far too mysterious and formless for their liking, especially if they are predisposed to the cut-

and-dried, precise, and definitive modes of so much modern technical and analytical thought (which has affected a large segment of the modern Church, where there is a sense that God can be definitively known). But lectio also refuses to be confined by the imaged side of the prayer continuum. It knows a God whose ways are not our ways, and about whom all language is only an approximation.

When lectio urges us to consider that God has a particular and unique word for each one of us, we must not imagine that we will hear a voice speaking in our ear, saying something like "turn right at the next intersection"! The conviction that God cares about us and is so involved in our lives as to respond to our calls with guidance does not mean that God has been reduced to our size. But it does mean that we can be helped by a power greater than ourselves, if we are willing to consider the possibility in terms we do not necessarily understand and certainly do not control. Such an approach is remarkably similar to the modern spiritual phenomenon of twelve-step groups based on the Alcoholics Anonymous insight that there are inner chambers in all of us that do not yet believe in and trust a power greater than ourselves. In certain secret compartments, all of us share the pain of the man who cries, "I believe; help my unbelief!" (Mark 9:24).

One of the most pressing issues of human life has to do with the experience of great trials that seem to be in contradiction to the gifts of a loving God. These trials may be so personal and so close that we think of them as trivial compared to what others suffer, and yet they are for us very difficult to bear. Trials can include suffering a chronic disease or handicap, or having to endure an overly demanding or critical boss or a gossipy next-door neighbor. Watching one's children as young adults make self-destructive choices is a trial. Trials might involve the slow recovery of memories of childhood abuse, trusting that in time healing will come, or gathering the courage to leave a present abusive situation. Struggling to learn to love honestly, when everything in one's background teaches one to hate or when one has been divorced by an unfaithful spouse, is another trial. Trials might also involve caring for an ungrateful parent or a retarded child, or the personal agony of working in a humiliating environment or a thankless job.

The fact is that when we live with our eyes wide open to the actual situations of our lives, it is very difficult also to believe in the call each of us has to holiness. Yet we do—each of us—have such a call, and at some level we know it. There is a deep, maybe hidden, inner longing to share in God's life, to know ourselves infinitely precious, to be embraced in the loving union of absolute wordless understanding with the Great Other. At some level of ourselves, each of us can get in touch with this call when we are quiet. And here God meets us, just as Christ met Matthew, the "sinner," and went to dinner with him, coming generously to those who know their need (Matthew 9:9–13).

Yet it is often very painful to know our need, to believe in the irresistibly attractive invitation of God to be the very beloved. It is painful to believe in this, like touching one's hand to a hot fire, because even as we recognize it, we also know how great is the distance between our weary and often irksome daily round and that mysterious grace to which we are called.

We usually do what we can to hide from one side or the other of this double truth. We close our eyes to the reality and live in an interior fantasy world, telling ourselves that the present suffering is only temporary illusion. Or we close our ears to the call and embrace of God, telling ourselves that if God really were calling us to such a state, real life would be different. We may think it better to believe in no God at all than to suffer the tension between what we long for and what we have.

The process of lectio on life invites us actively to live into both sides of this double truth: both the reality of the hard trials we must endure *and* the reality of our personal call to holiness. When we do this, we somehow participate in the blossoming forth of God's Kingdom, for which we daily pray. God somehow awaits and then uses our willingness to be stretched between these apparent contradictions to do the work in the world that is the Kingdom's present fulfillment. On reflection, we realize that Christ Our Lord did just this work of living into both sides of the double truth, as did his mother. We also are invited to this work. This is the formative perspective of lectio, which integrates life and prayer.

Group Practice of Lectio on Life

With this background, we turn to the practical question of how to practice lectio on life. What specific method can help us more fully to integrate our prayer and our life, our trials and our call? How do we begin to express this perspective and this willingness in our actual life settings? How do we read the "texts" of life in lectio? Here we explore one method, using a continuing example.

The pattern of lectio on life follows that of basic lectio:

Prepare.

1. Hear the word. Review recent life events and select a single incident for reflection.

2. How is my life touched? Review the incident mentally and emotionally, as it happened, then be receptive to a phrase or image that seems to be given in relation to it.

3. Is there an invitation here? Offer the incident and your reflections back to God, then rest and be responsive to an invitation that might come.

4. Pray.

As with lectio divina, lectio on life can be practiced alone or in a group. In a group practice, the time required may be somewhat longer than that for lectio divina, because of the somewhat more directive and explicit guidance involved, and the somewhat deeper level of intimacy required. The group process is described below, as we look at each of these steps in turn.

PREPARE

The group members gather and sit in a circle. The leader invites the group to begin with a recollection process. Each person takes a comfortable but alert position, closing the eyes and concentrating on breathing. Exhalations are used to release tension and preoccupations; inhalations are used to receive God's presence here and now. The group members gradually let their thoughts die away, seeking to be fully present in this moment.

EXAMPLE

The group from Immanuel Church has been meeting for nine months, and has decided to try a lectio on life this time. The meeting is at the home of Mary and Bill, and Charles is the leader. As before, all six gather and settle food, children, and themselves. The group has asked the babysitter to stay a little longer this time, as the lectio on life practice may take a little longer than usual.

Charles officially convenes the group, and leads them in a time of preparatory quieting, reminding everyone to sit comfortably, close their eyes, and center themselves with breathing for several quiet minutes.

STAGE ONE: HEAR THE WORD

The leader invites the members, still with their eyes closed, to review mentally the events of the last few days or week, gently and attentively "turning the pages" of their recent life experiences. The aim is simply to recall what happened day by day, or hour by hour. And, as memorable moments come to mind, gradually let each memory pass through your awareness. After a time, perhaps it will seem that one event or situation seems to recur again and again in your thoughts. Perhaps one moment seems especially to seek greater attention and reflection.

Each member takes time to decide on one particular incident, and then holds it gently in his or her mind. After a few moments, the leader brings the silence to a close, and invites the members one by one to state simply the approximate time of day when their chosen incident occurred. Each one states a time and that is all.

EXAMPLE

Charles speaks, encouraging group members to think over the events of the past several days, just letting each situation flow through the mind, and finally allowing one particular incident to come to the fore. After two minutes of silence, he asks each person to share (or pass) by simply speaking aloud the approximate time of day when the remembered incident occurred. He begins, saying, "9:00 A.M." Jim says, "2:00 P.M."

Ann says, "I have one incident at 12:30 and one at 6:00 A.M.; how do I choose?" Charles smiles and says, "It doesn't matter; either will do. Just go with one of them." Ann decides, "12:30."

Sharon says, "10:00 A.M." Bill speaks, "about 6:00 P.M." And Mary says, "I'm not sure—about 2:00, I think."

STAGE TWO: HOW IS MY LIFE TOUCHED?

The leader now invites the group to return in thought to the chosen incident, this time exploring the question "How is my life touched by this incident?"—understanding now that *touch* means particularly *touched by God in Christ*. The leader begins by asking members, with their eyes closed, to review mentally the physical aspects of the incident, to recreate it vividly and sequentially in their minds, recalling colors and shapes, textures, smells, sounds, and so on. About two minutes of silence is given for this exercise.

Asking that members continue to keep their eyes closed, the leader encourages each one now to recall the incident emotionally, looking especially for the places where the strongest emotional energy (positive or negative) is experienced, and any moments of noticeable energy shift. About a minute of silence is given to this.

Now the leader invites the members to set aside the specific incident for a moment, letting their minds be blank, if possible. This setting aside of the memory creates an expectant and receptive interior space, into which a word of blessing or consecration is invited. So, with a free mind, each person allows a phrase or image that seems somehow related to the chosen incident to surface unconsciously. The phrase or image may be from scripture—a phrase from one of the Psalms or an incident in the Gospels, for example—or any favorite book. The person does not need to understand the reason that the image emerges nor its connection to the incident. Each one just lets some phrase or image come into his or her awareness. About two minutes of silence is given to this.

Finally, the leader reminds the participants that the image or phrase they have received is a kind of blessing or consecration of the incident, a sign of Christ's presence in it. They are now invited to share *briefly* only the phrase or image they have received. In just a sentence or two, each person may describe the discovered phrase or image of blessing (not the life incident), beginning with "I hear" or "I see." As before, it is always permissible to pass.

EXAMPLE

Charles asks the group members to close their eyes and relax, now mentally recalling the selected incident in some detail, trying to recreate in as much sensory detail as possible exactly what happened: sights, sounds, smells, and sequence of events. After about a minute, Bill starts to say, "It was last Thursday . . . ," but Charles quickly says, "We don't share the specifics out loud now, Bill. Just stay with your memories in silence for now." At the end of two minutes, Charles encourages everyone to keep their eyes closed while he gives a bit more guidance.

He encourages them to continue reflecting on the incident, going back over it again in terms of their feelings during the occurrence. He asks participants to let their feelings flow in sequence, as they did at the time, noticing particularly any sharp rise or fall in energy, and pondering what was going on when such energy shifts occurred. He asks for continued silence during this further reflection.

After another two minutes, Charles asks everyone just to relax, setting aside all thought, and being open to any image or phrase that comes. It might be a person (say, Abraham) or a phrase (say, "Oh God, help") or maybe a favorite image from any book (say, Fiver's vision in *Watership Down*). The members simply wait quietly, ready to receive some phrase or image somehow related to the incident they have been pondering. When the image or phrase is received, each person just holds it quietly in mind.

Charles gives about two minutes of silence for this, and then encourages everyone to understand the image or phrase as a sign of Christ's presence in the incident. He then invites members to share in a sentence or two the image or phrase received, suggesting they might begin with "I hear" or "I see."

There are several more seconds of silence. Finally, Sharon says, "The image I get is not from scripture; it's of Brother Lawrence with his arms up to his elbows in soapy dishwater!"

Jim says, "I see Jesus in the wilderness with Satan; I don't know how that can be a blessing."

Mary says, "I hear the verse from Psalm 42: 'My soul longs for you like the deer for streams of water.'"

Bill says, "You all know the scripture better than I do. The image I got was of Huckleberry Finn, sitting on the edge of a river with his bare feet dangling in the water and a piece of straw hanging out of his mouth. Now that's a blessing!"

Ann says, "This shifting around is pretty confusing to me. I pass."

Charles says, "I see Jacob waking up and realizing that God was in the spot where he slept, and he had not known it."

STAGE THREE: IS THERE AN INVITATION HERE?

When all have shared or passed, the leader again asks the members to center themselves, remembering Christ's active presence in their midst and resting in that presence. Then the leader asks them to close their eyes again and bring back to mind *both* their life incident and the image or phrase associated with it. They are asked to place, in their imagination, the incident and their reflections on it into an offering plate and lift the plate up to God, placing on top of the offering the image or phrase that came to bless it. Each person is to offer everything connected with the incident to God—any insight, any confusion or pain, any unresolved feelings—all are offered back to God now. You offer what was done, what was not done, what might be done—giving all back to the Giver of all things. It might help to give a big exhalation, physically letting it out. About one minute of silence is allowed for this.

When this action of offering is completed, all are invited to rest as peacefully as possible in God's all-embracing presence, content for a time to be with God without comment. Let this silence last about one minute.

Finally, the leader encourages the group to be receptive to any invitation or encouragement that may seem to be given in relation to all that has been pondered. Does the incident, after reflection, suggest an invitation to be or to do something in the next few days? Or does the image or phrase that surfaced carry with it an invitation? Perhaps in the offering to God some sudden insight emerged. Or possibly in the silence and rest, a word of encouragement or hope seemed to appear. Taken together, does there seem to be here an invitation to be or to do something in the next few days? This is pondered in about two or three minutes of silent reflection, and then the leader asks everyone to share their invitation, or to pass. Sharing may be at somewhat more length this time, and each person pays particular attention to the sharing of the person to the right.

EXAMPLE

Charles draws the group back into silence again, asking that each person bring fully back to mind both his or her incident and the image or phrase that blessed it. Everything is to be placed imaginatively in offering and lifted up to God. If anyone needs to hold some part back, that is all right, but they are all to try to give everything connected with the incident and their reflection on it back to God. The image or phrase they received is settled on top of the offered incident as a sign of blessing, a sign of Christ's presence in the incident, and all is handed over to God. Charles encourages members to make a loud sigh of exhalation to express their offering, as if saying, "Here, God, take it now!" After that, he tells them, there will be a time of sitting quietly in silence, resting in God. Charles gives a total of about two minutes for both elements, the offering and the resting.

After the two minutes have elapsed, Charles asks the members to stay in their inner silence a little longer, especially receptive now to any invitation that may be given in connection with their lectio on life. In the quiet, does any invitation come to be or to do something in the next few days? Might that invitation be expressed in words? Charles gives another two minutes of silence for this.

Drawing the silence to a close, Charles asks the group to share now a few sentences about what each one feels invited to do or be as a result of this reflection. Anyone may pass, but those who wish are asked to share their invitation.

Bill says, "Boy, it's pretty clear to me that I'm being invited to lay back a little in the next few days, just to relax and get my bare feet in the water, so to speak. If Mary's game, maybe I'll take Wednesday off and drive up into the mountains!"

Mary says, "I'd love to, Bill, and I'm due for a little time off. Maybe we can find a running stream with a deer beside it! I think my invitation is to be with God a little more, so possibly we could each kind of wander on our own, and then come back together to share a little of what we discovered?"

After a moment, Ann says irritably, "The incident I remember was a terrific fight I had with my mother on the phone last week, and it upsets me a lot to remember it. She never listens to me, and she's always putting me down. I can never win with her. And I don't know why you made me remember it, when it brings up so much pain for me!"

Sharon reaches out and squeezes Ann's hand. After a moment Sharon says, "Some days I feel so depressed, and my incident involved such a day. But the image of Brother Lawrence finding God in the soapsuds made me laugh inside, and I began to feel an invitation to find God in *all* the things the day brings—both good and bad. I can't imagine how to find God in depression, but this week I plan to look."

Jim starts to say something, then stops and is silent for a few seconds. Finally he speaks, "There is something funny about this whole process for me. You all know that I have stuck with it only because I love you, and I've wanted our group to continue meeting. But it's weird. I mean, I used to feel quite certain about things; everything about my faith was black and white. And now so much seems fuzzy. And yet somehow, that's not bad! There is a peace in my heart that I never felt when everything was so clear intellectually.

"In the past, even with my faith in God, I still felt responsible for everything; I felt I had to make things happen. But now I feel I can occasionally trust things to God . . . not all the time, mind you, but now and then! And I see why the image of Jesus with Satan is really a blessing to me. In response to Satan's temptations, Jesus keeps saying, 'I place myself under God the Father's will and power; no matter how gifted I am, the main thing I do is put God first above all.' And I see that way of being as an invitation to me in my life now."

Charles says, "Sometimes I feel like Rip van Winkle, just waking up from a long sleep. Everything around me seems so alive, so vivid, these days. On my way to work one day last week, it was as if suddenly I woke up and really heard the bird song and saw the marvelous color of the autumn leaves and smelled the fresh, crisp air. . . . It was all so wonderful, I felt speechless! Young Jacob really had it pegged: 'God is in this place, and I did not know it!' That's my invitation right now—to stay awake.

STAGE FOUR: PRAY

When all members have shared or passed, the leader asks each person to pray for the person to the right, praying that person will be empowered to be or to do what he or she has sensed as invitation. Everyone is asked to pray, although anyone who wishes may pray silently. At the end of each prayer, the one praying says "Amen," and it is repeated by the group. When all have prayed, the group does not immediately get up, but allows a few gentle moments for the transition back to ordinary life interactions.

EXAMPLE

Charles continues, "Each of us will pray for the person on the right, asking God to make possible our response to this invitation. We all join in the Amen each time. I'll begin.

"God, I do pray for my sister Mary and for the deep longing in her heart for you. I ask you to help her set aside some time for you in the next week, and to know that she is as loved and cared for by you as any creature of the forest. Amen." All respond Amen.

Mary prays, "Father/Mother God, how much I thank you for my husband Bill, and for his growing willingness to play with you and me and the kids. I pray especially that you will tickle his feet with water and warm his back with sun and generally be so inviting to him that he delights this week to set aside time for you. Amen." All respond Amen.

Bill prays, "Heavenly Father, I ask you to continue blessing our sister, Sharon. She is such a source of warm caring to us that I pray you will help her receive in abundance both our caring for her and your care for her. Especially be with her the next time she feels depressed, and let her know you are there. Amen." All respond Amen.

Sharon prays, "Our God, be with my friend Ann. I know how hard she struggles sometimes to keep her head above water, and how much she has to overcome. Do embrace her in her pain; do bring her healing. Amen." All respond Amen.

Ann says, "I'll pray silently." She takes Jim's hand in both of hers, and bows her head for a minute or so. Then she says "Amen," and everyone responds Amen.

Jim looks moved, and continues to hold Ann's hands, but turns his body toward Charles, and prays, "God, you know how much I love this guy, and how much of an inspiration his simple faith is for me. I think he's plenty awake, but I know he longs for more, and so I pray you'll keep giving him more and more of yourself, and help him to keep sharing that with us. Amen." All respond Amen.

The group members look up and smile shyly at one another, stretch a bit, touch each other briefly, and gradually move out toward the family room for supper.

Summary

The description and examples here have presented a means of using our life situations as texts for lectio reflection in a group process. The process may seem a bit cumbersome at first, as is any new discipline, such as tennis or playing the piano. Gradually the group will become accustomed to the pattern, and it will flow more easily. The chart that appears at the end of this chapter can be used as a leader guide, to aid the flow in early practice sessions.

Lectio on life is a very powerful process because we are intentionally bringing to God the broken and confused places in our lives for healing. Sometimes very painful or old memories can surface, and these may be difficult for both the individual and the group. As in lectio divina on scripture, the basic principle is to trust in the healing and embracing presence of God in one's midst. However, in general, this is not a substitute for those who are (or need to be) dealing with crisis stages in psychotherapy.

Our incarnational principle encourages us to accept the wisdom of using the skilled resources available to help us heal both physical and emotional wounds. While prayer is always part of this healing, it is unnecessary to trust prayer as the *single* resource, without the supplement of those natural and human means through which grace ordinarily works. The psychotherapy now available is potentially an enormously helpful resource. Whenever we feel consistently depressed, confused, or unable to cope with life issues, we may wish to consider exploring that resource. You should be aware, however, that there are a great many practitioners, not all of whom have been carefully trained or licensed. If you decide to seek this kind of help, it is well to get referrals from people you know and trust, either a friend whose therapist has proved helpful or a member of the clergy whose discernment you respect.

Help can be sought for a variety of coping issues, on a much wider range than was once the case. At present, for example, many skilled helpers practice in the areas of ordinary marriage and family issues. At the other end of the scale are highly trained professionals who work with those suffering from severe psychic burdens such as multiple-personality disorder and schizophrenia. In particular, if and when the supportive intimacy of a lectio community seems to bring to the surface deeply troubling material, it is only sensible to consult a professional or pastoral advisor to determine whether therapeutic assistance could be helpful.

Sometimes, as we gain strength through the prayerful support of loving Christians, old issues will begin to surface in lectio on life as expression of our readiness to work with these issues in therapy. Or we may already be in therapy, and find prayer an essential support for the healing of memories, as in lectio we explore how God was actually present to us in ways we did not then realize. Always, the best support we can give one another is our ongoing love and care, and our entrusting of those we love to God, who is doing for them more than we can ask or imagine. Lectio is designed to help us learn to do this for ourselves and one another, in all times and places. May you be so blessed!

CHART 2

The Process of Group Lectio on Life

The group lectio on life process includes these steps, slightly elaborated to assist the leader in such practice.

Prepare.

1. Hear the word.

Review recent life events and select a single incident for reflection.

Give several minutes of silence for reviewing the hours and experiences of the last several days and allowing one event or situation to keep returning for attention.

Ask group members to state simply the approximate time of day when their chosen incident occurred.

2. How is my life touched?

Review the incident mentally and emotionally as it happened, then be receptive to a phrase or image that seems to be given in relation to it.

Remind group that "touched" refers to the touch of Christ.

Ask them to recreate the incident as it actually happened, remembering all they can about sights, sounds, etc. Allow one to two minutes for this.

Ask them to recreate the emotions of the incident: Where was the strongest energy or any major energy shift? Allow one to two minutes for this.

After two or more minutes, ask them to set aside mentally all their musings, and let their minds be receptive to a phrase or image from scripture or literature.

After two minutes, remind them to be aware that the given phrase or image is a blessing, a sign of Christ's presence in the incident.

Ask group members to share only their phrase or image.

3. **Is there an invitation here?**

   Offer the incident and your reflections on it back to God. Rest and be responsive to an invitation that might come.

Ask group members to bring back to memory their life incident and their image or phrase alongside it. Allow one minute to hold both in peace.

Urge them to offer everything mentally up to God, to let it go for now.

Ask them to be receptive to any invitation or encouragement that may come now to be or do something in the next few days. Allow about one or two minutes of silence for this.

Invite members to share their invitation.*

4. **Pray.**

   Pray for the person to the right.

Afterwards, the group may share how it went, if desired.

---

* Note: Anyone may pass at any time.

CHAPTER 6

The Judeo-Christian Heritage of Lectio Divina

We are commended to the practice of lectio as a central tool of Christian faith by two quite dissimilar sources. On the one hand are the sources of the past, rooted so deeply in the Christian heritage that it is likely Jesus himself practiced something like lectio in his earthly life. On the other hand are the sources of the present drawing us into the future, springing up in modern Christian practice wherever the Church is at its liveliest and most relevant, so close to the emerging vitality of Christian growth that it seems certainly a central manifestation of the Spirit of God. This chapter describes some of these sources. The developed forms are slightly different, but both past and present sources clearly suggest what we have come to recognize as lectio: that slow, contemplative interaction with Scripture that brings union with God and sinks into one's own heart as the ongoing, vibrant spring of new life.

Scripture Itself Invites Lectio

THE PASSAGES

Scripture itself draws us to lectio. This is particularly true of the poetry and wisdom literature in the Psalms and Proverbs, for example, but it can be found throughout Scripture, and especially in the mature spiritual reflection of the community of faith. Periodic shifts in language and translation sometimes tend to obscure references to lectio in Scripture, but let us look closely and consider the invitation that emerges.

> When I was a [child] with my father, tender, and my mother's favorite, he taught me, and said to me, "Let your heart hold fast my words; keep my commandments and live." (Prov. 4:3–4)

Over and over in the Psalms and Proverbs we encounter this kind of invitation: "My child, listen with the ear of your heart!" The parents are responsible to give the child not only the gift of life, but the ongoing gift of knowing how to *live*. And the secret of this gift of life is that our heart "hold fast" to the words that are given. "Hold fast" and "keep" are terms inviting us to ponder, to reflect, to turn something over and over, until it becomes part of our very being. The offered words or commandments are not the arbitrary words of one human father, but are rather the wisdom gathered by the whole community and generally expressed in the written tradition. Indeed, these words are the words of God, the words of life.

At crucial points in the Scripture, we find major actors practicing just this exercise of reflective lectio. Abraham, David, and Mary are key examples. Take, for instance, the passage where God makes a covenant with Abraham, promising that he will be the ancestor of a multitude of nations, specifically through a child of his and Sarah's:

> Abraham fell on his face and laughed, and said to himself, "Can a child be born to a man who is a hundred years old?" (Gen. 17:17)

The most literal translation is that Abraham "laughed in his heart," and the implication of the word "heart" is that he is taking this promise of God into his being, keeping it or turning it over in a reflective way, and thereby somehow cooperating with the transforming power of God. As we have seen, the human heart is the locus of our capacity for cooperating with God, the locus of our capacity for lectio.

David, dedicating and crowning his son Solomon, summarizes the wisdom he has inherited from his community and manifested in his reign, in a consecrating prayer that embodies the lectio approach:

> I know, my God, that you search the heart, and take pleasure in uprightness. . . . Now I have seen your people, who are present here, offering freely and joyously to you. O Lord, the God of Abraham [and Sarah], keep forever such purposes and thoughts in the hearts of your people, and direct their hearts toward you. (1 Chron. 29:17—18)

Again we notice the central scriptural terms "keep" and "heart." The terms in this prayer invite not merely a passive acceptance of God's purposes, but rather an intention toward active engagement, meditating on and interiorizing the word of God.

To keep a thing is to care for it tenderly and to turn it frequently. God's law is to be savored like precious grains, root vegetables, or pots of honey that are stored away in a safe place and regularly examined and turned over so that they might be kept as a ongoing source of nurture. Everything comes from God, but we have an obligation of good stewardship to care for these gifts. And a major means of care, especially for the most valued gift of the word, is to "store up" or "treasure."

In the New Testament, there are two central passages in which Mary, the mother of Jesus, keeps something in her heart. Both these passages occur in the second chapter of the Gospel of Luke. In the first, immediately after Jesus is born, Mary and Joseph are visited by the shepherds telling their story and praising God. We are told that Mary "treasured all these words and pondered them in her heart" (Luke 2:19). Mary regularly returns to examine and turn over these words, carefully tending something precious that it may nourish her. This work is done in her heart.

Later on, when Jesus is twelve years old (the year he becomes a man), the holy family goes to Jerusalem for the festival of Passover. This time Jesus stays behind and is lost to them; the parents must return to Jerusalem and undertake a long search, only to find him in the temple, which he calls "his Father's house." Again we are told that "his mother treasured all these things in her heart" (Luke 2:51).

Somehow in the midst of these perplexing yet important events of her life, Mary is using her heart to reflect, or we might say she is doing lectio. And the suggestion is that her willingness to do this somehow enlarges her already mature capacity to respond to God and continue to be a contributing part of God's purposes in the world.

Indeed, as we become sensitive to the way lectio finds expression in human life, it is not difficult to find many of Jesus's sayings as the fruit of his own practice of something like lectio. Consider for example the answer Jesus gives to John the Baptist when John sends from prison to ask if Jesus is "the one to come." Jesus responds to this painful inquiry from his cousin and longtime friend in this way:

> Go and tell John what you hear and see: the blind receive their sight, the lame walk, the lepers are cleansed, the deaf hear, the dead are raised, the poor have the good news brought to them. And blessed is anyone who takes no offense at me. (Matt. 11:1–6)

Will this answer comfort John? Yes, indeed! And why? It takes a little research to make the connection, but it is well worth while. Jesus is clearly referring to passages in the Hebrew Scriptures, Isaiah 42:6–7 and 61:1, in his answer to John. He is evoking the image Isaiah presents of the Messiah as Suffering Servant. Of all those persons closely connected with Jesus in the Gospels, only John gives evidence that he *shares* this vision of the Messiah, the one to come, as Suffering Servant. Indeed, John has described his own ministry precisely with reference to this same vision of Isaiah of the Messiah as Suffering Servant. He calls himself the "messenger, . . . the voice of one crying out in the wilderness 'Prepare the way of the Lord'" (Mark 1:2–3). This language, too, is taken from the prophet Isaiah, appearing near the passages Jesus later returns in gentle and affirming answer to John (Isa. 40:3). Is it too far-fetched to imagine Jesus and John as adolescents, poring together over their Scriptures lectio-style, and finding in the words of Isaiah the ideas that later emerge in their individual and mutual sense of vocation?

THE WORDS THAT CALL OUT

We have discovered two key words used in Scripture to suggest what we have called lectio. These words commend a devotional, personalized, and imaginative approach as a means of taking inward and making personal the objective truth of the Word. The "code words" of Scripture alerting us to a practice of lectio are *heart* and *ponder* or *keep*.

The *heart* is the locus of the person's capacity for this work of keeping things, which is the work of lectio. God's people are to "give thanks with the heart" (Ps. 138:1), to have courage in the heart (Ps. 27:3), to "seek God with our whole heart" (Ps. 119:2), and above all to have "a clean heart" (Ps. 51:10) and to be "pure in heart" (Ps. 73:1). Hannah's heart rejoices (1 Sam. 2:1), and David grieves in his heart (1 Sam. 21:12; 27:1). Things kept or turned over in the heart seem to evoke the transforming power of God, whether they are kept with delight or sorrow!

The Greek word *symballo* (*ponder*, in English) literally means "cast together," suggesting the major metaphor for lectio scriptural devotion, which is *keep*. Precious goods are cast together or stored up, creating a treasure that is kept with care. In this sense, to keep (or ponder) a thing means to set it aside along with things that seem somehow similar to it, to turn all these things over in one's mind with some frequency, and to value them according to their ability to provide the nurture required for life.

Such keeping involves a keen sense of stewardship of real material things, while also acknowledging the sense in which they are *a gift*. In just this sense, David keeps the sheep (1 Sam. 17:34), the people of Yahweh are to keep the covenant (Exod. 19:5), and the King himself is to keep the law (Deut. 17:19). Likewise, in the New Testament, Mary ponders and keeps these things in her heart (Luke 2:19, 51), deepening the mysterious interaction of event and promise in her life.

Occasionally, Scripture evokes the lectio process with the word meditate, as when Isaac wonders about a bride (Gen. 24:63) or a righteous person considers the law (Ps. 1:2). But lectio's work of interiorizing the word of God is usually referred to with the more lively notion of keeping or pondering something in one's heart. Jesus calls us repeatedly to "hear the word and keep it" (e.g., Luke 8:15; 11:28), meaning that we are to practice what we call lectio with God's word as revealed in Scripture and life, in order that the Word might abide in us. And the final book of the Bible, Revelation, begins and ends with a benediction for those who hear (the word) and keep it. (Rev. 1:3; 22:7, 9).

Historical Usage and Development of Lectio

HEBREW ROOTS

There were two main methods of Scripture study used by the Hebrews, one of which was called *halakhah*, meaning adherence to traditional rules of spiritual practice having a legal character (e.g., the Ten Commandments). The other method was called *haggadah* (or *hag-*

gah, for short), meaning a narrative, imaginative, and interactive interpretation of Scripture. This second method involved using stories, legends, and folklore to amplify a Biblical passage for devotional development. This haggadah "is intended to bring heaven down to the congregation and also to lift them up to heaven."[1] It involves several levels of textual study, from the literal to the mysterious, via the free use of text to explore its inner meaning.

This method is observed frequently in rabbinical commentaries on Scripture, and was probably a part of the devotional practice of ordinary Jews in Jesus's time. The words of the Torah, or law, were to be interiorized by the faithful. They were memorized in a process that involved repeating passages over and over softly with the lips, until the words themselves gradually took up residence in the heart, there transforming the person's life. The human relation to God's law was one involving *all* aspects of one's being: mind, body, spirit. Thus the phrase, "learning by heart," had a vastly different value in ancient Hebrew practice than the generally superficial meaning we currently assign it.

This Hebrew method is quite similar to the favorite method of Bible study in the first five Christian centuries called *allegorical*, which involved meanings literal, moral, and eschatological (pertaining to the end of time). Christian monastic practice of lectio divina was a later offshoot of the allegorical method as well as Biblical and Hebrew sources.

EARLY CHRISTIAN CENTURIES

Another important influence which shaped the early practice of lectio was the practice in Greek and Roman secular schools of *meditari*, which means the active visualizing of an event in order to prepare for it mentally before it happens. For example, the fourth century John Cassian attributes to Abbot Nesteros these words to a new novice:

> If only you will transfer to the reading of and meditation upon the writings of the Spirit, the same diligence and earnestness which you showed in those secular studies of yours . . . it will come to pass that not only every purpose and thought of your heart, but also all the wanderings and

rovings of your imagination will become to you a holy and unceasing pondering of the divine law.[2]

This passage suggests that even the secular approach to reading taught during these centuries involved a type of mental and emotional integration, which when applied to the particular words of Spirit-inspired Scripture, can become a life-changing experience.

Yet the practice of lectio among literate Christians in the first centuries of Christianity was not primarily dependent upon secular sources. Indeed, as early as the middle of the third century we find letters among Christians writing of lectio practice:

> Be constant as well in prayer as in reading; now speak with God, now let God speak with you, let Him instruct you in His precepts, let Him direct you.[3]

We can see here that rhythm of activity and receptivity in prayer—or of life integrated with the Word of God—that is so characteristic of the practice of lectio, and observe that it seems to be the standard means in that time of relating to Scripture. We notice particularly that lectio divina was so common a practice in the third century that the word we now translate as *reading* was the term describing what we understand as lectio.

Lectio divina has been generally known as the Benedictine approach to Scripture, because it is so characteristic of the Rule of St. Benedict (written about 525 A.D.), and subsequent centuries of monastic practice under the Rule. Indeed, in chapter 48 of the Rule on daily labor, he spelled out a pattern of community prayer, manual labor, and reading (lectio) that formed a balanced set of activities for growth incorporating all aspects of our humanity. In this pattern, lectio practice was to be undertaken for about four hours each day!

Lectio was so common a practice among Christians of his time that Benedict did not even feel the need to describe how to undertake such a central activity. However, it clearly involved those elements that have emerged as central throughout our discussion, although the specific format may have been somewhat different than that suggested in this book. Yet lectio always involves a slow, meditative reading of the word, balanced with periods of silent reflection. It is both active and receptive. It is not principally oriented toward the gathering of information, but rather toward a personal encounter with the living God that casts light on present life issues. It is a way of bringing the Scripture to heart, of making its promises one's own in a transformed life.

In Benedict's time, the primary practice of lectio was personal, but lectio also formed a principal means of attentive worship in the eight daily gatherings for common prayer, which centered on the Psalms. The root of this lectio process is found in Benedict's conviction that God calls out the invitation for a deeper loving relationship to each Christian each day.[4] It is largely the Benedictine monastic tradition that has kept alive this precious treasure of lectio practice through the intervening centuries.

Perhaps we can understand somewhat more fully what the monks, nuns, and oblates were doing in their practice of lectio, if we read a few lines from the twelfth century work of Guigo II the Carthusian, called *The Ladder of Monks*. In this work he attempts to provide a systematic analysis of the various stages or steps in the lectio divina process. Guigo writes to his brother Gervase that in pondering "our spiritual work," it occurred to him that it might be considered in four stages. In lyrical prose, Guigo calls these four stages (1) reading (*lectio*), (2) meditation (*meditatio*), (3) prayer (*oratio*), and (4) contemplation (*contemplatio*). Clearly he is using all four of these terms rather specifically. What he says is this:

> Reading seeks for the sweetness of a blessed life,
> meditation perceives it,
> prayer asks for it,
> contemplation tastes it.

> Reading, as it were, puts food whole into the mouth,
> meditation chews it and breaks it up,
> prayer extracts its flavor,
> contemplation is the sweetness itself which gladdens and
>   refreshes.[5]

For Guigo, the practice of lectio is the practice of a soul on fire with longing for the Loved One. It is the response of a soul to the powerful attractiveness of the One for whom we were made. But lectio is not only the expression of longing on the human side, it is also one of the means by which God's very self "breaks in upon the middle of our prayer, runs to meet us in all haste, . . . and restores our weary soul."[6] It is a way, in short, in which God draws us into God's own life. A beautiful aspiration is shared over the centuries, along with one method of practicing it stepwise!

REFORMATION EXPERIENCE WITH LECTIO

Words tend to change with worldviews, and we may find it difficult to trace lectio through the tumultuous period of the Reformation and the Counter-Reformation. Although it is clear that some reformers sought to do away with everything monastic, we can also trace through language shifts a careful keeping of the lectio mode of personal engagement with the living God in some of the reformers' new language and in their personal practice with Scripture.

For example, Martin Luther's "How to Read the Holy Bible" suggests an approach congruent with lectio method, in which Luther himself would have been spiritually formed. He asserts that the foundational principles of "reading" the Bible are these: first, humbly to implore God for enlightening grace, always bearing in mind that the Spirit-inspired word can only be understood by the Spirit presently in our midst; and second, to bring a mind free from ideas and a heart eager to know and do God's will. Although Luther explicitly argues against the emphasis on allegory in Catholic teaching of that time by asserting the importance of never deviating from the literal meaning of the text, he also confesses awareness that the language of biblical authors often has special meaning that is hard to understand, and urges that the key to understanding is always to seek to find Christ even and especially in the Old Testament passages, which is, of course, an allegorical approach.[7]

It is clear how parallel these elements are to our practical mode of lectio practice: Our lectio method emphasizes the role of silence as a means of being open to the Spirit. It focuses on seeking Christ's presence as we ponder how the passage touches us. And it is oriented to-

ward the heart as the responding center as we consider an invitation offered by the passage.

John Wesley, in his "Advice for Spiritual Reading," also suggests
guidance remarkably parallel to the lectio process:

> Be sure to read, not cursorily or hastily, but leisurely, seriously, and with
> great attention; with proper pauses and intervals, and that you may allow
> time for the enlightenings of the divine grace. To this end, recollect, every
> now and then, what you have read, and consider how to reduce it to prac-
> tice. . . . Read those passages over and over that more nearly concern
> yourself, and more closely affect your inclinations or practice. . . .
>
> Select also any remarkable sayings or advices, and treasure them up in
> your memory; and these you either may draw forth in time of need . . . or
> make use of.[8]

Wesley urges slow reading with pauses in which to be receptive to
the invitations of the Spirit, just as does our lectio process. He asks
us to consider these invitations, whatever they may be, in practical
terms, "consider how to reduce [them] to practice," or we might say,
how to integrate them in our daily lives. He too suggests the importance of the heart as the primary place of response, emphasizing that
memorization is a means of receiving the Scripture that God's life
may transform us from inside. So, even in the turbulent development
of new denominations in the Church, even across periods of dramatic
shifts in language and approaches to Christian experience, an emphasis survives on devotional presence with Scripture for spiritual
growth. And that emphasis strongly parallels the method presented
here for group lectio.

Modern Developments

At one pivotal point in the New Testament, Jesus is told by the
Pharisees to make his followers be quiet, which is in effect a demand to
shut down the growing faith in him as the Son of God. His response
is this:

> I tell you, if these [people] were silent, the stones would shout out. (Luke
> 19:40)

We have seen that the practice of lectio divina has been central to Christian devotional practice throughout the centuries. Yet because of its identification with monastic practice, it more or less went underground during the Reformation (sixteenth century), and has gradually fallen into disuse since the Enlightenment (eighteenth century). Recent centuries have been much more interested in approaching the Bible with the mind than with the heart, and we have not known how to integrate what our mind tells us about Scripture's gradual human evolution with what our hearts long for in terms of union with God. However, we can take comfort from Jesus's assurance that important things cannot be suppressed by arbitrary authority. As a powerful means of direct encounter with God that gives new hope for daily life, lectio is now bursting forth again in a groundswell of Christian experience, in widely diverse places. The stones are shouting out the invitation to encounter God in Scripture through this simple method! New forms of lectio are blossoming forth in our own day in a number of Christian settings. Let's look at some of these.

AFRICA

In South Africa, the Catholic bishops have established a religious education center called Lumko, which has developed an immensely popular Bible-study method widely in use among new communities of Christians. Their model has seven steps that are directly parallel to the model offered in this book, which forms the modern basis for the details of our lectio practice. Those seven steps are as follows:

1. We invite the Lord.

2. We read the text.

3. We pick out words and meditate on them.

4. We let God speak to us in silence.

5. We share what we have heard in our hearts.

6. We discuss a sense of what we are called to do.

7. We pray together spontaneously.

This model is explicitly oriented to the life problems being experienced by members of the group, with an intention to set God's word in Scripture alongside those problems to see what insights are revealed. And it is profoundly community oriented: Life problems include not only personal ones, but also those of the whole community as they share work tasks as well as prayer life. The sessions always end with two explicit questions:

"What does God want us to do?"

and in response,

"Who will do what and when?"

There is in the Lumko method a keen sense of expectancy that God is living and active, directly concerned with the people's lives, and specifically guiding and empowering certain communal actions. And the process explicitly includes the practice of lectio on life, discussed in chapter 5, in which the basic text involves life incidents as well as Scripture passages.

LATIN AMERICA

In Latin America also, a new approach to Bible study has been developed. This approach, presented in a book called the Gospel in Solentiname, shares some aspects of lectio but includes other elements. In this method, communal commentary on the Scripture is substituted for the homily in the mass. The emphasis is not so much on what the gospel *should* mean as on what it *does* mean to the illiterate and poverty-stricken faithful. It is very parallel to lectio in its emphasis on personal expectant listening, eager to hear God's word in the Scripture in a way that will give help for the vital struggles of daily life.

In the Solentiname approach, both the confidence in the Spirit's presence with the hearer, which enables reception of the Word, and the insistence that the living Word will always be in dialogue with concrete life issues, are closely parallel to our lectio practice. There is a deep conviction that Jesus lives and is present among those who call on him, mixed with awareness that the community of people is the *Body* of Christ, and therefore given to each other for mutual comfort and care.

This very strength of communal sharing also suggests the disparity between the Solentiname approach and the lectio model, which is that the former focuses less on personal application and meaning and more on wider disorders of the social and political context. However, it must be said that this broader social emphasis has for cultural reasons given just the personal sense of empowerment and value that it is hoped the more personal emphasis will give to those using the lectio method presented here.

THE UNITED STATES

The headquarters office of the Episcopal church of the United States has adopted a practice of Bible reflection like lectio and has begun using it particularly in its evangelical training. Lectio is so meaningful that it spreads like wildfire, such that a recent meeting of all the Episcopal bishops in the United States used this Bible reflection as part of their daily sessions, as a means of centering on their common faith in a time of considerable conflict on specific issues. International meetings of Christians are finding lectio a centering component, especially where highly diverse constituencies are dealing with a welter of anguishing problems. The 1992 Women's Conference in Latin America used a daily lectio-type Bible-study format, as did the 1989 international Lambeth Conference of Anglican bishops.

The Roman Catholic church in the United States has used a lectio-like practice extensively in its Rite of Christian Initiation for Adults, the catechumenate for adults. The rite draws on the church's African and Latin American connections, as well as on a process offered by American Jesuits called *collatio*, or shared meal. Collatio is actually a shared praying on Scripture in a format very like the one we call lectio. That format also calls for three separate readings of the Scripture, with plenty of time spent in silence, and a sequence of shared contributions. Sharing is kept very short and personal, emphasizing the personal meaning of the words and spontaneous prayer. The Jesuits call the process collatio because it is composed of everyone's contributions, and thus brings forth a nourishing creation centered in the word of Scripture.

Summary

In this brief survey of modern developments in lectio, we see the tremendous hunger for an encounter with the sacred Scriptures that is life bringing. This hunger is evident among rich and poor, clergy and lay, across all denominations and many continents. What is perhaps most amazing is the similarity between the methods chosen by many diverse movements of Christian people throughout the world as they turn to the Bible devotionally and for empowerment. And the similarity of practice crosses not only the barriers of space, but also those of time. We find many elements in common among all the approaches.

It is hoped that the particular model of lectio offered here will be an aid in the already strong movement of God's people reading God's Word, inspired by God's Spirit.

Epilogue: The Example Group After One Year

Throughout, this book has presented group lectio as an instrument of gradual transformation. We come in expectancy to our group lectio, experiencing our longing for God as well as our personal dilemmas, seeking somehow an integration of these two important aspects of our lives. We might reasonably wonder what transformation into Christ looks like. We don't all expect to be saints or monastics, so what *will* our lives be like, as we open them increasingly to the formation of the Holy Spirit?

As a partial answer to these questions, this chapter provides an imaginary gathering of our sample lectio group after they have been meeting for a little over a year. The group has already had its annual evaluation meeting, and all six have decided they would like to continue together in the same format for another year. This meeting is a bit after that one.

EXAMPLE

The group has gathered and settled in. Ann is the leader for tonight, and she has selected Hosea 2:14–15a for the Scripture. She makes sure the chairs are in a circle, and takes some time to connect by word or touch with each member present before the group convenes. She has been praying all week, and is somewhat nervous about leading, but she feels confident in this small group of supportive friendship, so she is willing to see what happens.

When everyone is sitting down, Ann says, "I always like the first few minutes of our meetings best—when I come in a little tense and anxious, and we all just take a few minutes to be together and relax and remember Jesus is here. So let's do that now for a few minutes—remembering to check our posture and our breathing and to soak up the loving care we all bring for each other in this moment." There is a little shuffling, and then silence for a few minutes.

Then she says, "Listen now to the Scripture. I'll read it twice, at first just for you to hear it overall, and then a second time more slowly, for you each to hear your own special word. The passage is from Hosea, chapter 2:

Therefore I will now allure her; I will bring her into the wilderness and speak tenderly to her. From there I will give her her vineyards, and will make the Valley of Achor a door of hope. There she shall respond as in the days of her youth.

There is about a minute's silence, then Ann says, "Okay, now let's each just say the word or phrase from the passage that seems to speak to us. Mine is 'a door of hope.'"

Jim says, "In the days of youth."

Charles says, "Into the wilderness."

Mary says, "Her youth."

Sharon says, "Tenderly."

Bill says, "Allure."

Ann nods in acknowledgment, and then asks Jim to read the passage the second time, handing him the Bible. She says, "This time we hear the Scripture, we are listening with the question in mind, 'How is my life touched by this passage?' We remember that touch may be sensual, like a picture or a sound, or it may just be a connection we notice. Listen now, and in the silence after the reading."

Jim reads the passage, and Ann consults her watch so that she will know when two minutes will have elapsed. Then she closes her own eyes in meditation.

At the end of two minutes, she says, "We can share now how we sense our lives touched. Just a sentence or two, beginning with 'I hear' or 'I see.'"

After a few seconds, Charles begins, "I'm thinking about what the wilderness is for me. I used to think of it as a barren place, but since I've been backpacking regularly in the desert, I've come to appreciate its subtle charms. I feel there is a parallel somehow in my life, with its mix of barrenness and unexpected blossoming."

Mary says, "My youth . . . I have a sense of such carefree lightness. . . . I miss it."

There is a silence, then Jim says, "Youth means something different for me, I think. When I was a kid, I was very serious. I get a picture of this little owl with glasses on! That was me." He laughs ruefully.

Bill says, "You know, I almost feel Jesus tempting me, if you can say that. It's like he's pulling on my heart, saying 'love me'—almost erotically. Wow, it's like I desire to be with him more than anything!" He looks embarrassed.

Sharon says, "I see our little daughter with the neighbor's big old dog. He always treats her with such infinite patience and care. It's almost as if he knows his own great strength, and even when she accidentally hurts him, he never strikes out at her."

Ann says, "I hear music; it seems to come from somewhere far off—both vocal and instrumental, with haunting beauty. And even though it is far away, it is wrapping around me and enfolding me in delight. It's almost like I live in it, just as a fish lives in water all around." She pauses, then says, "All right, let's hear the passage now a third time," she passes the Bible over to Mary, "and this time we'll listen especially for an invitation which seems to be here for each of us, something to do or be within the next few days or week."

Mary reads the passage again, and Ann lets three minutes elapse this time before speaking. "Now we may share for the third time. This time we can speak a bit more if we wish, and we are sharing what, if any, invitation seemed to come to us from the passage for our lives right now. Anyone is welcome to pass if you wish. Remember to pay special attention to the one sharing on your right."

Mary says, "As I myself read the passage, I heard something I had not heard before. It is not just a recalling of the days of my youth with nostalgia; something else is happening here. It is God loving and giving and bringing into being something *for me*—something as lovely as youth, but even better. It is not just fixing something broken, but some new wholeness that goes beyond what was possible then. And I think the invitation for me is to relax and let God do things in me that I can't do for myself. . . . Um, specifically, I feel I'm being invited to take a couple of hours during this week to do something just for the pure pleasure of it! I don't necessarily have to fight for pleasure; maybe I can just flow with it, when it's given!"

Bill grins at her. "Amen to that! I have this funny and kind of unsettling impression that I'm being invited to enjoy and honor my *desires*! That sounds so weird, but what I mean is that, uh . . . I keep going back and back to that question Jesus asked me in our first meeting: 'What do you want?' And every time I answer it, it's as if I go deeper and deeper inside myself. What I really want is to be with Jesus, all the time. Gosh, words are so awkward!

"Anyway, the impression I have is that Jesus himself puts that desire deep in my heart, and is almost alluring me to let him be first in my life. And as I let that happen, there's kind of a difference in everything. I'm enjoying Mary and the kids more, but I'm less demanding of them. I'm taking a day off from work now and then, and I'm actually finding that in being less compulsive about work in general, I'm enjoying it more. Not that it's all roses, by any means—the economy is still rotten, and my boss is still a stickler for detail—but you know, it's fun now! I guess my invitation is to keep having fun. Wow, that sure doesn't *sound* like a spiritual discipline, does it!" He grins again and shakes his head.

Charles says, "That's sort of what I'm feeling too, Bill, but also a little different. Like Jim, I've always been a kind of serious guy, and I'm always trying so hard to figure things out. But you know, I just begin to think I've got a handle on something, and they change the rules on me. I've been driving myself crazy trying to keep on top of everything. For example, the way I've been glued to public television these last few days, you'd think they couldn't run the Congress without me! So anyway, it's been real good for me to begin paying more attention to the physical world, and to my body—like with camping in the desert. I've been noticing things I never saw before, and for me that desert really is a place of hope. I watch the seasons change, and the tiny blossoms that appear given the least little encouragement of water, and there's a sense of continuity and peacefulness that's just great. I feel real good about myself—I've even lost thirty pounds! . . . My invitation is just to keep at these simple things that I know are so good for me, even for my soul."

Sharon says, "For me those simple physical things—the flowers in the meadow, the hot soapy dishwater, the children and animals—always have been important, but it's almost as if they are deepening in importance now.

My main work right now seems to be mainly to engage seriously with this depression, and to face the truth of my childhood abuse. And sometimes that is overwhelming in its pain and its power. But often when it seems just too much, a sunbeam will glance through the kitchen window, almost like the finger of God tenderly plucking on the strings of my heart, and I feel the sudden bittersweet delight of simply being alive! So for me the invitation is to trust in the tenderness, to believe that God is like the neighbor's dog—improbable as that sounds!—and that the power is always tempered by loving care for me."

There is another pause, and then Jim says, "On this last reading, I heard a new word that had not struck me before, and that was 'vineyards.' I have always been particularly attracted to the image of Israel as God's vineyard, or God's grapevine, and for years I have appreciated the historical metaphor of the grapevine in Psalm 80. You remember that in that psalm, Israel is crying out to God, asking why he allows the vine (themselves) to be trampled underfoot, when he previously planted them and cared for them so tenderly. It is an impressive feat for the psalmist and prophets to come up with the understanding that their country was suffering so much war and looting because the people had defaulted on their covenant with God and depended on their own strength."

Jim glances over at Ann, clears his throat, and is silent for a moment. Then he says, "What I am trying to say is that when I was a youngster, I always felt that I was God's favorite, that I was specially chosen. And that's not necessarily a bad thing. It's just that I started feeling so responsible, to be singled out like that and given so many blessings. I began to think it was my job to set everyone on the right track, and to fix everything. And this ongoing problem with Ann's mom has just set me on my tail. That woman baffles me; she just won't listen to reason. She's irrational, and nothing that I can do makes the slightest impact on her. Meanwhile, she's wrecking our lives! But it's the oddest thing. Somehow the fact that I couldn't fix it for Ann—or for me—has made me realize all over again, like I haven't felt since I was a kid, how very much I need God. And I've prayed like I haven't prayed for years—really *needing* God's help. It's not that everything has miraculously cleared up, though it is a little better. But I feel a whole lot better. Thanks to you all I know I have help, and that's good. So I just need to keep asking for help."

There is a warmly shared silence. At last Ann says, "For me, these days, there is hope. Jesus still seems far away, but through you friends and our time together, I suspect that he is near, too. My invitation is just to hold on to that hope. Or maybe better, to keep opening that door just a little bit more whenever I can. . . . Dear friends, let's pray together."

Everyone bows their heads, and Ann takes Jim's hand. "Jesus," Ann prays, "thank you for Jim. I pray that you will fill all his needs. Amen." All echo Amen.

Jim prays for Bill, "Father, thank you for reaching into Bill's heart and letting him know that you gave your Son because you love him and the world so much. I pray you will keep him in the happiness of knowing that, deep in his being. Amen." All say Amen.

Bill prays for Sharon, "Lord, we grieve that our sister has to suffer so much pain, but we trust that every day you are bringing her some healing. Let her continue to see your tender care each day in some gift of the day. Amen." All say Amen.

Sharon prays for Charles, "Our God, be with my husband, who is so often aware of his own barrenness, even when others of us see mainly his wonderful blossoms. Thank you for helping us to share this love of nature. Amen." All say Amen.

Charles prays for Mary, "God, you have given Mary the gift of bringing to all around her so much joy; do give her those special couple of hours with you this week, and let her relax into the joy you would give her. Amen." All say Amen.

Mary prays for Ann, "Mother God, tenderly take our friend Ann into your embrace in a way that she has never known, and let her be nourished and strengthened in your bosom. Amen." All say Amen.

Ann says, "Let's all say the Lord's Prayer together by way of a closing blessing." And they do.

In this example we see that transformation into Christ looks perfectly ordinary. In Christ, we do not stop being the people we are; we do not float around like angels. We bring the fullness of our personality, and we also discover an increasing richness of life previously only glimpsed. Problems do not disappear, but we have a better perspective on them, and we can value and receive the genuine help available to handle them. There is a sense of greater balance and wholeness in our lives, and an awareness that pain and joy are both part of the gift of being human.

Our thirst for a deeper life in God does not diminish, and may indeed increase. But our thirst is matched by a sense that we are also receiving regular and satisfying spiritual refreshment and strength for the journey. We feel part of a whole people of God, living and dead, in whose support we are strengthened. God's life in us becomes a practical resource, accessible and fruitful in the living of our ordinary lives. The Word in us is prospering, and so are we. God bless us all in this journey of spiritual growth through Bible reading.

Notes

INTRODUCTION

1. The primary source for lectio divina is monastic experience, especially as required by the *Rule* of St. Benedict of Nursia, who makes lectio a substantial element in each day's schedule. He wrote the *Rule* about 525 A.D. and it has formed the basis for Christian monastic practice since then. See *The Rule of St. Benedict in Latin and English with Notes*. The translation of the *Rule* by Timothy Fry, O.S.B., Senior Editor (Collegeville, MN: The Liturgical Press, 1981) or my own commentary on the *Rule* called *Preferring Christ*, which has a translation of the *Rule* by Luke Dysinger, O.S.B. (Trabuco Canyon, CA: Source Books, 1991).

CHAPTER 2

1. Carl Rogers, "Some Elements of Effective Interpersonal Communication," cited in John Mallison et al., *Building Small Groups in Christian Community* (West Ryde, NSW, Australia: Renewal Publications, 1978), 128.

CHAPTER 5

1. C. S. Lewis, *Letters to Malcolm: Chiefly on Prayer* (New York: Harvest/HBJ Books, 1964), 75.

CHAPTER 6

1. See Isador Singer, ed., *The Jewish Encyclopedia*, vols. VI and VIII, especially the article on the "Midrash Haggadah" (New York: Funk and Wagnalls, 1904), 349.
2. John Cassian, *The Conferences*, vol. XI, The Nicene and Post-Nicene Fathers (Grand Rapids, MI: W. B. Eerdmans, 1986), Conference 14, p. 441.
3. St. Cyprian of Cathage (d.258), "Letter to Donatus."
4. *The Rule of St. Benedict.* See especially verses 9–13 of the Prologue.
5. Cistercian Studies Vol. 48, 68–69.
6. Ibid.
7. T. A. Readwin, ed., *The Prefaces to the Early Editions of Martin Luther's Bible* (London: Harchard and Co., 1863).
8. Frank Whaling, ed., *John and Charles Wesley: Selected Writings* (New York: Paulist Press, 1981).

Additional Resources

This is a list of books you may wish to consult for additional information on the practice of lectio divina and the related topic of group dynamics.

de Mello, Anthony. *Sadhana: A Way to God.* St. Louis: The Institute of Jesuit Sources, 1978 (especially Exercise 33, pages 107–111).

Dysinger, Luke, O.S.B., "Accepting the Embrace of God: The Ancient Art of 'Lectio Divina'." *The Valyermo Benedictine* 1 (1):33–43.

Hall, Thelma, R.C. *Too Deep for Words: Rediscovering Lectio Divina.* New York: Paulist Press, 1988.

Hestenes, Roberta. *Using the Bible in Groups.* London: The British and Foreign Bible Society, 1983.

Leclerq, Jean, O.S.B. *The Love of Learning and the Desire for God.* Translated by Catharine Misrahi. London: SPCK, 1978 (especially Part One, "The Formation of Monastic Culture" and Chapter One, "The Conversion of St. Benedict").

Michael, Chester P. and Marie C. Norrisey. *Prayer and Temperament: Different Prayer Forms for Different Personality Types.* Charlottesville, Va.: The Open Door, Inc., 1984 (especially pages 31–45).

Mulholland, M. Robert, Jr. *Shaped by the Word: The Power of Scripture in Spiritual Formation.* Nashville, Tenn.: The Upper Room, 1985.

Muto, Susan Annette. *A Practical Guide to Spiritual Reading.* Denville, New Jersey: Dimension Books, 1976.

Panimolle, Salvatore, ed. *Like the Deer That Yearns.* Middlegreen, Slough, England: St. Paul Publications, 1987.

Pennington, Basil, OCSO. *Monastic Life: A Short History of Monasticism and Its Spirit.* Petersham, Mass: St. Bede's Publications, 1989.

Pennington, Basil, OCSO. *Light from the Cloister.* New York: Paulist Press, 1991 (especially the chapter entitled "Listening").

Saint Benedict, the Rule of: in Latin and English with Notes. Timothy Fry.
O.S.B. (ed.), et al. Collegeville, Minn.: The Liturgical Press, 1981 (especially chapter 6, "The Role and Interpretation of Scripture in the Rule of St. Benedict").

Smith, Martin. *The Word Is Very Near You: A Guide to Praying with Scripture.* London: Darton, Longman, Todd, 1990.

Wiederkehr, Macrina, O.S.B. *A Tree Full of Angels: Seeing the Holy in the Ordinary.* San Francisco: Harper and Row, 1988.